ADVANCE PRAISE

*"Like many male leaders in Corporate America, I didn't know what I didn't know. Not just about women's issues, but also about all the things that male leaders pay no attention to on a daily basis—such as sexism, bias, and white male privilege. Through an extraordinary set of circumstances, I have spent a significant amount of time during the last 15 years focused on women, business, and leadership—and why this is a business imperative. Bonnie and Jessica's book (Un)Skirting the Issues: A Guide for the Well-Intentioned Man in Today's Workplace leverages a healthy dose of humor and storytelling to explain in no uncertain terms why engaging men in this imperative is essential today."*

JEFFERY TOBIAS HALTER, PRESIDENT OF YWOMEN, AND
AUTHOR OF *WHY WOMEN: THE LEADERSHIP IMPERATIVE
TO ADVANCING WOMEN AND ENGAGING MEN*

"What happens when you don't know what you don't know? Nothing good. That can be especially true on the job. Even some of us males who think we are gender sensitive and advocates for women in the workplace are quite capable of stubbing our toes...to say nothing about failing to improve the workplace systemically. Fetch and Poliner have created a helpful guide for both genders. And with lots of humor in the mix! Very helpful indeed!"

PETER BRUCE, FORMER EXECUTIVE VICE PRESIDENT, NORTHWESTERN MUTUAL LIFE INSURANCE COMPANY

"Riveting read—and a must for anyone in business. Bonnie and Jessica have found the hidden gem in driving equality in the workplace! The book is a perfect summation of the challenges women, especially ones in leadership roles, face as they work to stay on the same playing field as their male counterparts, while bringing the next generation of female leaders through the ranks. The book sets itself apart from the rest by exploring alternative solutions that we, as a society, can do about these challenges to support women in the workplace and drive higher ROIs for companies."

HEATHER SULLIVAN, SENIOR MANAGER, ACCENTURE

"This book felt semi-autobiographical, reminiscent of stories I have traded with girlfriends. Jessica and Bonnie do a great job of capturing experiences women in high- level positions in the corporate world face every day. This book will not only be a conversation starter, but both men and women will appreciate the practical advice."

LATASHA GILLESPIE, GLOBAL DIVERSITY
AND INCLUSION DIRECTOR, AMAZON

"How do we fix workplace cultures so the most talented people get to do their best work? The authors draw on their rich experience to offer many wise and practical approaches to rid organizations of sometimes unconscious, but always corrosive assumptions."

DAVID BRANCACCIO, HOST OF PUBLIC RADIO'S
MARKETPLACE MORNING REPORT AND TELEVISION HOST

"After several years of leading women's initiatives in the corporate world, I am thrilled to see a book for men about gender in the workplace! The authors' real-life examples spur readers on a path of self-reflection, and the practical tips incite change. I often read inspiring stories of female role models to my two young daughters and encourage them to be their authentic selves, but tackling gender bias can't just be the role of women, real change will happen when we are all receptive and committed to building an inclusive environment."

AMANDA GRAHAM, CATERPILLAR INC.

"It's about time we have women write a book that doesn't tell us how to fix ourselves, but rather addresses those male colleagues who understand that women's struggles in the workplace are about how to better share leadership. Thank you, Jessica and Bonnie."

"Thanks to the authors, who have realized that involving men in the quest for gender equity is a good thing. After all, we are part of the problem in the first place. Yet better still, the authors move on to practical and tested advice on how to make a difference in the workplace today. A useful book for those who want to achieve gender equity in the workplace."

"This book is a timely and thoughtful examination on how the work of gender equality is shared by us all. Specifically, it adds to a burgeoning literature which suggests that as women progress through the workplace, the conscious sponsorship of the well-intentioned man is a necessary part of success, particularly in male-dominated cultures, such as finance, technology, manufacturing, engineering, and law."

*"Some of my earliest memories are of drawing pictures with neon yellow, green, and orange highlighters under my family's breakfast table. The context for these drawings is the reason (Un)Skirted and its topic, the success of women in the professional workforce, is personally important to me. The markers belonged to my mother, who entered law school in 1972, when I was less than two years old. She was one of three women in her class. Three years later she finished first in that class. But because no reputable law firm in Oklahoma City would hire a female associate at that time, she scrambled to find a job. When she found one as an in-house lawyer for Kerr-McGee Corporation, she was hired by a 'well-intentioned male' general counsel who also saw an opportunity to get great talent cheap. In-house pay was about half of law firm wages for (all male) associates. The refrain offered most often for this disparity was that men had families to feed. And yes, my mother had a husband who was himself an attorney and who did provide for our family. As my mother's son, however, this excuse for her half-pay always rankled me. Despite the hours she worked, the sweat equity she expended, and the valuable counsel she delivered, her hard work was somehow deemed less valuable than that of my father.*

*Today I see few workplace cultures that have evolved into the gender-inclusive environments that I imagined for my mother when I was a child. I wonder how I, as a general counsel and a well-intentioned male, can help. Creating an environment of gender equality takes work. Hiring and promoting women is a start. Including women in enrichment opportunities, leadership programs, and as decision makers at every level is critical. This book is a considerable resource to myself and others, who are genuinely well-intentioned, but do sometimes fall short of the mark, as we chart a path toward parity in the workplace."*

JAMES M. (BUDDY) ROBINSON IV, SENIOR VICE
PRESIDENT—GENERAL COUNSEL, CORPORATE SECRETARY
AND BUSINESS DEVELOPMENT, KOHLER COMPANY

*"By enlightening and challenging the 'well-intentioned male' to help his women colleagues succeed, Jessica and Bonnie give hope that the professional woman's star can rise alongside her male colleagues."*

NADELLE GROSSMAN, DIRECTOR, ASSOCIATE LAW
PROFESSOR, MARQUETTE UNIVERSITY LAW SCHOOL

*"Men play a critical role in addressing unconscious bias that still exists in today's workplace. (Un)Skirting the Issues explains how to identify these biases and effectively deal with them to strengthen teams and ultimately business performance."*

KARL WEISS, VICE PRESIDENT, CATERPILLAR, INC.

*"Jessica and Bonnie are able to address the unconscious bias that so many women face (and after working for almost a decade in HR, I can say that I have seen and heard it all) in an honest, amusing, and supportive way. What sets this book apart is that it approaches a topic that all managers, both men and women, need to learn more about, yet the authors are able to come at this issue directly and without talking down to their readers or assuming that there are bad intentions. This is the answer to every manager and HR representative who is looking to teach about a very real problem in a positive light with actual solutions."*

ANDREA, FORMER HR BUSINESS PARTNER

*Well overdue, (Un)Skirting the Issues flips the script on the typical women in the workplace narrative, asserting that men must contribute to gender equality in business. In an honest and thoughtful work, Fetch and Poliner reject the pervasive assumption that women must learn to assimilate to a man's world, arguing instead that men can be agents of change in creating successful co-ed work environments. A must read for the modern man who acknowledges women's value in the workforce and wants to attract and advance female talent.*

ELIZABETH LUEDER, INVESTMENT ATTORNEY,
OTTAWA AVENUE PRIVATE CAPITAL, LLC

# UNSKIRTING THE ISSUES

# (Un)Skirting the Issues

## A GUIDE FOR THE
## *Well-Intentioned Man*
## *in Today's Workplace*

BONNIE FETCH AND JESSICA POLINER

LIONCREST

PUBLISHING

UNSKIRTING THE ISSUES

*A Guide for the Well-Intentioned Man in Today's Workplace*

ISBN   978-1-61961-712-4  *Paperback*

       978-1-61961-713-1  *Ebook*

*This book is dedicated first and foremost to our families. Unconditionally loving and supporting two type-A workaholics is no small task, and you make us who we are today and better each day. This book is also dedicated to our dear friends who are the real deal. Spanning companies, generations, and the globe, you make us stronger, smarter, and funnier than we actually are. To our professional networks and colleagues, you are our daily reminder and inspiration to do what we do to build a more inclusive workplace for generations to come.*

# Contents

——

FOREWORD ..................................................................19

INTRODUCTION ................................................25

1. JUST THE FACTS, MA'AM .....................................53

2. SO, WHAT'S A WIM TO DO? ...............................73

3. SHE'S NOT WHAT YOU EXPECTED ........................83

4. SHE DOESN'T WANT A FREE RIDE ........................95

5. PLEASE LET HER FINISH ...................................105

6. WHY MUST SHE CHOOSE? .................................115

7. WOMEN CAN'T HAVE IT ALL, BUT THEY CAN DO IT ALL ..127

8. PROVE IT (AGAIN)...........................................141

9. IT'S NEVER THAT TIME OF THE MONTH ...............159

10. THAT'S ACTUALLY NOT A COMPLIMENT..............171

11. SHE'S NOT REALLY SORRY ...............................181

CONCLUSION ..................................................189

ABOUT THE AUTHORS......................................193

# un•skirt

___

*verb*

To engage, to dive into, to seek understanding.

*Ant.* To skirt – to avoid, go around the
edge of, or keep distant from.

*Rel.* Unskirted (*adj.*) – without a skirt.

# Foreword

## BY STEVE L. ROBBINS

———

When Bonnie and Jessica asked me to write a foreword to their book, I was honored and excited. I had never been asked to engage in such a task. And if you know anything about my life journey, you'd also know the issues they address in this book are deeply personal for me. Of course I would write the foreword! My intent was to author the best foreword ever written, one that would go down in the annals of great forewords.

At the time of their request, I was deep into my speaking season, crisscrossing the nation to give talks and workshops. Then one of my sons had a seizure. We continue to deal with the after-effects at the time of this writing. On top of that, another son was rehabilitating from hip surgery. As things progressed, I never completed the foreword in the time frame promised. These two wonderful people nudged me gently with e-mails to finish the foreword, even though the deadline passed. As I was about to let them know I would not be able to execute my task as promised, I reread the introduction to the book that they had previously sent. It hit me! I was one of the guys for which this book was written.

Many well-intentioned men (WIMs as Bonnie and Jessica refer to us) have great interest in women's issues. A good portion of our interest comes from the fact that we all have women in our lives that are, have been, or will someday be negatively affected in a world that's often implicitly and explicitly tipped in favor of men. Some of us men are unable or are unwilling to see imbalance. Others of us can't comprehend or admit that we were given an insider's compass for navigating a world that other men built, or should I say, got the bulk of the credit for building. Women tend not to get that compass or must pass a different set of tests and meet a different set of standards to have compass access. Note that I didn't say "get a compass," just temporary access to one.

Like myself, many of my male brethren do indeed get upset when we hear stories of unfairness, injustice, and plain discrimination. It's a heartfelt discomfort that makes visible the reality that many parts of our society and our workplaces are still unfair to and unjust for women and girls. But many times, our dissonance can't find its way past deep-felt negative emotion. We sympathize and empathize, but we often don't actualize.

There are many reasons for our inaction. Some are justified. Others can only be defended if we fumble a few facts or resist the truths contained in the realities others live. Our inaction, though, is not innocuous. Lack of action has effects. Those of us, with Y chromosomes, are not often burdened by the effects that women endure on a relatively regular basis. We have, as I term it, "insider privilege." Yes, funny as it sounds, we have the privilege of not recognizing we have privilege. And then we get upset when others tell us we have privilege, because of course, it's about talent and hard work. Reality check. Research into success says a lot of where one is in life is a combination of talent, hard work, relational networks, and luck. The largest factor? Luck!

So, I had great intentions of writing this foreword, but other priorities popped up. What I failed to fully digest is that Bonnie and Jessica had priorities too, and I had promised to assist them with theirs. If I didn't keep my promise, I would be doing, at a micro-level, what organizations and societies do at a macro-level. We promise to address women's issues, then, in short, we don't. In organizations, leaders (mostly men) will recognize gender inequality as an important issue in need of rectification. But then, amazingly, very little happens. Correction. A lot of things happen. Committees and groups are formed. Celebrations take place. Speakers, like me, are brought in to dispense words of wisdom. Then, little to no change happens in the substantive areas that actually need changing.

Let's change that men (and women). Let's do things that have meaning, that create lasting, meaningful change. I begin again by keeping my promise of finishing this foreword. You can begin or begin again by reading this book and by taking to heart the powerful words Bonnie and Jessica offer. Use their stories and suggestions to fuel and guide your next steps. And remember, it's rarely the one or two big things that are done that make change. It's the everyday, mundane things done over and over and over that slowly cultivate a new reality.

I leave you with some words of a woman I highly respect and greatly miss—my mother. When she noticed I tended to be selfish, looking out only for my own interests, she gently reminded me with these words, "You walk on a path cleared by others, so it's your responsibility to clear a path for others." Guess who cleared a path, sometimes

a wide path, for all of us. Women! Our mothers! It's pay-
back time!

STEVE L. ROBBINS, PHD, AUTHOR OF *WHAT IF:*
*SHORT STORIES TO SPARK DIVERSITY DIALOGUE*

# Introduction

---

Ask either of the authors about one of the most common phrases they've heard when meeting just about anyone in their industry for the first time, from colleagues, customers, suppliers, or distributors, and this is what they'd both say without hesitation, **"You are *not* what I expected."**

They've talked about it, and neither of them are completely sure what *is* expected. Apparently, though, neither of them meets expectations for a senior professional in the industrial business world. For both Bonnie and Jessica, it can get a little comical at times, and they've found humor to be a strong remedy. More than once, they've each been picked up at the airport by a driver in a foreign country wielding a sign emblazoned "Mr. Bonnie Fetch" or "Mr. Jessica Poliner." The immediate assumption is that, regardless of the name, a person with their professional title and responsibilities must be a man.

Jessica has been asked to get someone a cup of coffee or to make a photocopy, out of the assumption that she's the administrative assistant or receptionist. Likewise, when either of them is met for the first time by accomplished men, men who also manage teams and departments, men who've climbed to at least the same career level that they have, the expectation is somehow that they'll be older? In trousers? No makeup, no heels? Have shorter or greyer hair? Be less feminine? They haven't been able to put their finger on it, but they've both felt implicitly—or they've been told, explicitly, at times—that their femininity places them distinctly outside the mold.

Bonnie's career began before Jessica's, and she spent years steeped in an unconscious effort to assimilate. She was ambitious and determined to get ahead in a male-dominated environment, and that meant unknowingly changing herself and changing how she responded to others in an effort to demonstrate competence. It took years, but eventually she had an epiphany that her ability to blend in was getting her, and the women she worked with, nowhere from a gender-inclusion perspective. In an effort not to be seen as self-serving, she'd avoided advocating for women, and all she'd accomplished was to further entrench her workplace and her colleagues in the status quo. She realized that in order for things to change, someone had to speak up—and not just speak up, but model the behaviors and attitudes that were so dearly missing.

Jessica, more often than not, has been outspoken—she's passionate about the topic of gender inclusion in the workplace because she's witnessed the effects of the gender gap around her: the difference in gender pay, the different language used to reference women in career and performance discussions, and the number of smart, talented women opting out of the workforce or leadership. Jessica began her career as a corporate attorney in a law firm, an environment in which the gender gap wasn't as apparent at the entry level, but was still subtly present, especially in discussions of the "partner track." When she moved from in-house corporate counsel in technology and financial services companies over to the industrial world, and later from the practice of corporate and M&A law to leadership roles within various businesses, she simultaneously sharpened her EQ (emotional intelligence) on gender inclusion and grew more aware of her surroundings. The gaps in gender inclusion became more blatant to her.

At this juncture, it's important to highlight the obvious: women are complex beings (as Bonnie's husband reminds her regularly). While it may be improbable, if not impossible, to completely understand women, the authors have set out to help men to recognize and address the unconscious bias, stereotypes, and ingrained expectations that affect women in the workplace today. They'll do this by sharing stories, research, and a healthy dose of humor to compel men to understand, and advocate for much-needed change in the work environment that will benefit everyone. Fair warning: some of the stories will surprise or even shock readers. But rest assured, the stories highlighted are not one-off situations—they're situations that occur at an alarming rate, even in the current decade.

## THE WELL-INTENTIONED MAN

Along the way, the authors have both encountered men who see the same thing. These are men who are aware that there *is* gender bias and exclusion in the workplace and who notice the ill effects on their teams. They are men who want to be part of the necessary change, but who have either been cowed into silence, afraid of offending anyone by saying the wrong thing, or who have no idea what to say in the first place. The authors have distinguished these colleagues as an archetype referred to as a "Well-Intentioned Man" (WIM, for those who have grown to like acronyms as much as the authors do).

WIMs are the men for whom they've written this book,

and if you're reading it now, there's a good chance that you're a Well-Intentioned Man. Bonnie and Jessica feel passionate in the mission to lead women through some of the more challenging career situations that they've had to navigate, and they know that they're well equipped to give women the right advice from their countless and continuous experiences. However, they also see a significant additional opportunity: there's a huge knowledge gap out there when it comes to advice for *men*.

Most of the advice and literature out there is for women. How to dress, how to speak, what to keep under wraps— there's a whole genre of books out there meant to help women to assimilate, cope, and compete in a work environment designed by and built for men. Men and women alike have discerned that the environment itself needs to be rethought and redesigned. However, the vast majority of literature out there paints a picture of why *women* need to be the ones to change. The Well-Intentioned Man who wants to move toward gender equality has very little actionable advice to go on. He generally needs to rely on a female colleague to either bail him out when he gets in hot water or to pre-read his communications and role-play his counsel to make sure he doesn't land there in the first place.

The playing field needs to be more balanced. Gender equality is the destination at the end of a long road, but what this book talks about is a step before that: simply, gender inclusion. Women need to be included in the conversation. They need to be included in considerations at every level, or the shape and flavor of the professional landscape will remain squarely male-focused. Women need to be included, and they need Well-intentioned Men to include them.

### MOVING THE NEEDLE

The authors first met each other and formed a connection based on a mutual desire to help women personally and professionally in their workplace. Truth be told, Bonnie reached out to Jessica to better get to know this high-potential, younger woman in her company and to see her in action. Very quickly, they realized the power of collaborating with one another. They'd both taken on a mentoring and coaching role with friends and colleagues in the past, and together they recognized the specific need that exists within companies to enhance the confidence, assertiveness, and business navigation skills of female colleagues. Madeleine Albright's famous quote—"There's a special place in hell for women who don't help other women"—is always at the forefront of their minds. Jessica, especially, grew up around driven, strong, smart women, and so helping to raise up other women and pay it forward has been a natural extension of her upbringing.

Even with the beneficial results they've seen from their

individual coaching, however, both of them have realized that all the coaching sessions and support in the world, woman to woman or through a multitude of conferences, panels, books, and events, isn't going to be enough to engender the kind of change needed in the workplace. Men must get involved, and women need to involve them in a meaningful and respectful way. Many companies are now aware that they need to make gender inclusion a priority, but the results aren't happening fast enough. Part of this slow pace is the sheer size and complexity of today's corporations. For companies with locations that span the globe, it takes a long time for lasting initiatives to ripple out from the epicenter of the organizations. To date, most of the momentum has been generated by women. Jessica and Bonnie know that they can help this shift happen with what they call "inverse support"—education and support for men who want to be part of the change, and even for men who don't yet realize that they *can* be part of the change.

Jessica and Bonnie's aim is to give Well-Intentioned Men the insight and advice to get involved in this effort, to start moving the needle, and to truly accelerate change.

## BONNIE'S STORY

When Bonnie began her career, she was in assimilation mode. She believed that she wasn't successful in spite of being a woman; rather, she was simply successful. She figured she must have been able to break through the glass ceiling she'd always heard about, and that was that. She was interviewed for books about professional advice she'd give her daughter, and she was sought after by other women for career coaching.

It wasn't until she was interviewed several years ago specifically about the gender gap that her perspective and attitude shifted. She was asked about the lack of women in senior leadership and if she had any ideas about how to close that gap. It was at that point that she began to realize that, while she had been successful, she'd gotten there at the cost of her own identity. She looked back on pivotal moments in her career and realized that she'd been assimilating to succeed, not succeeding and paving the way for other women to succeed. What's more, she'd been completely unaware of what she had been doing.

One day, Bonnie's husband asked her a simple question, "Why are you always the only woman in group pictures? Whenever I see photos of your coworkers, a customer visit, or a supplier visit, I don't see other women." He was just asking out of curiosity, but he'd identified the elephant in the room.

She began to question herself. Why weren't there more

women in leadership? Why wasn't she doing more for women? When it came down to it, while she was always willing to give women advice, she was afraid that actively advocating for women would look to others like she was advocating for herself. But by *not* advocating for women, Bonnie was hurting herself and other women in the long run. She was allowing her company to stay in a rut that was holding it back from being the best it could be. She was helping to groom an environment in which her own gender was not viewed as equal.

She asked herself, if *she* wasn't willing to be an advocate, then who would? When *would* she be willing to stick up for her own gender, if not now? She lit upon a new purpose: she wanted to help to create a working environment where women didn't feel like they couldn't do things. That sounds simplistic, but that's really what it comes down to. Women aren't on the outside because of physical *exclusion*— there's no bouncer at the door keeping the ladies out. But within the average workday, not to mention bigger events, there are dozens of smaller instances of women not being included in basic considerations.

Her first experiences in advocating for women at work found her pushing up against resistance from the women themselves. She had to push them, and push them hard, to get them to put themselves out there with assertiveness and drive. Once she showed them that getting in the room was not only possible, but essential, they were able to admit that it was something they'd always wanted but had assumed it was beyond their reach. This fired her up; here was her motivation, the knowledge that women *do* want to be part of the conversation, but they've been conditioned to believe that they never will be, and therefore they shouldn't try.

Bonnie has daughters and granddaughters. There is no reason that they should ever have to run up against any of this in their careers. That's her motivation: to speed up the change and to make her experience a relic of the past.

All throughout her career, she's had the opportunity to work with great men. She has male colleagues who perceive the gender gap and want to do something about it. She has other colleagues who have said male-biased things, and after a discussion, they can see and understand where they went wrong. She's had the benefit of watching the change that both authors are looking for actually happen person to person, one at a time. She wants to offer Well-Intentioned Men a rundown of practical things they can do to help change the conversation. She wants to give men actionable advice to make the workforce more gender inclusive.

## JESSICA'S STORY

In Jessica's career to date with different companies, industries, geographies, and professions, when it comes to most
of her daily interactions, there are usually very few women
around. Bonnie's story about being the sole female in group
pictures was one of the first commonalities they bonded
over; Jessica is almost *always* the only woman in the picture.
It still amuses her when the photographer awkwardly tries
to figure out where he should position her in the picture
so that she doesn't stick out like a sore thumb.

Jessica has worked with women who tell her that when they
are out in the field with their male counterparts, covered
in mud and sweat, and when the men are handed towels
to wipe off, somehow there appears a little pink towel for
the woman to use. She too has received her fair share of
pink and purple swag and T-shirts so large she could wear
them as dresses. She has even been gifted lipstick. She has
become accustomed to standing out and has watched other
women around her feel the same and has shared these
experiences with them.

Jessica has led predominantly male teams in her traditionally male-dominated industry, in many cultures
where women make up a fraction of the workforce. She
has worked hard to attract, develop, and retain women in
her organizations, with some success stories. She came to

industrial manufacturing with fresh eyes, and the benefit of prior experience working in industries and professions where the bias isn't as overt and where the gender imbalance is less stark. Bonnie came to the realization of that bias over the course of more than a decade; however, Jessica came to that realization much more quickly and with the resolve to do something about it *now*.

Jessica focused on grassroots efforts to shine a light on the need for gender inclusion. Her list of efforts is long. She created and sponsored internal conferences on women in leadership, she founded and then served as the executive sponsor for employee resource groups, she attended countless conferences, she served on panels and did speaking engagements, she developed personal brand and other self-development and realization courses targeting women (and also open to men), and she formally and informally mentored dozens of women and men. Yet Jessica realized that even with all the grassroots work, coaching, sponsoring, and speaking that she and others could offer, the pace of gender inclusion is still too slow. She now wants to attack the problem at a higher level, speaking directly to the men in leadership whose involvement is essential to spur this movement.

From the start, Jessica was influenced by two resilient and intelligent women: her mother and her maternal grandmother. Both of these women demonstrated through their countless examples and life experiences how Jessica could be strong, driven, and speak her mind. They cultivated her spirit (something they arguably regretted during her teenage years). Through a multitude of educational and professional moves as Jessica has grown, she assembled a robust global network of female friends across industries, professions, and walks of life, all of whom she admires and leans on deeply.

She was also fortunate to grow up surrounded by strong men who pushed and supported her as a smart, capable, hardworking *person*. They buoyed her as a confident athlete and a determined workaholic. There were no gender boundaries in their eyes, and Jessica does not recall any childhood memories of "feeling like a girl" in any plausible inferior sense of the expression. Growing up, she gained an invaluable lesson from her executive dad: he always said, "We all put our pants on the same way." It's something that she's carried with her, even when what she's putting on is a skirt.

Jessica has been fortunate as well to be mentored and sponsored by work heroes: intelligent, business-focused, creative men. She can't think of nearly as many women who have played that role in her career to date, unfortunately. Yet despite this strong upbringing and being backed with early professional success and with extraordinary drive and ambition, Jessica still suffered a crisis of confidence as she grew in her career. She straddled the double bind of competence and likeability as she ascended in leadership and broadened her experiences. She didn't see herself fitting in to the typical stereotypes of success with her company.

To combat these feelings of inadequacy, she devoured self-help books and focused on developing her self-awareness and EQ. She strived to see herself as others saw her. She wanted to be a well-liked, admired, and smart leader. At one point as she worked her way through her own catch-22 and 360 reviews, she realized, however, that it wasn't *her* that needed fixing; it was the organizational culture and the bias that permeates it.

Where Jessica hopes to get to is a place where women in leadership aren't atypical leaders, perceived as going against the norms of leadership *or* those of femininity. She wants to be viewed in a dress and possibly heels, without hesitation, as smart and likeable. She strives to overturn the unfounded lack of confidence she sees in many women that she mentors. She wants her women colleagues to have the confidence to assert themselves, to take risks, and to be their authentic selves—even if that means embracing a soprano voice.

Jessica knows that many of the men she works with don't

really see her, or her few female colleagues, as females, and these men are surprised to hear about the differences in treatment women face in the workplace. They simply see Jessica as a strong, smart, hardworking leader who cares about her people. Many don't recognize the unconscious bias that infiltrates the workplace. This book is for these men, who are asking for personal and professional guidance, and who know it's too important a topic to get wrong or to delay further.

## UNCONSCIOUS BIAS

When it comes to gender inclusion in the workplace, it's easy to see the *what*, but harder to pinpoint the *why*. There's no one with a clipboard at the boardroom letting men in and telling women they're not on the list. Instead, there's an unconscious bias toward a male-oriented status quo, as that's how it's always been. It's the big things, like the limited number of women at the executive level. It's the little things, too: the countless after-work happy hours or business social activities involving swimsuits.

Both authors are in a field that's male dominated. Jessica recalls that, as a lawyer, these signals of unconscious bias and aligning with a male-designed workplace were more subtle. They took more time, and bigger rocking of the boat, to really come to the surface. In the industrial world, you can find yourself anywhere from a boardroom to traipsing around a job site, covered in dust and sweat. It doesn't even require acknowledgement of the multitude of stares: women stand out.

Here's another small, but incredibly common, example. Both authors have experienced being in a meeting where a male colleague asks, in reference to an event, "Do we need to wear a coat and tie?" Both of them answer this question with the same tongue-in-cheek response, "I hope not, because I don't own any."

This may seem like small potatoes. It may seem like they're nitpicking language, or finding reasons to get offended. In fact, they rarely get *offended*, because it's hard to get offended about things that happen at such a high frequency. But they do notice these small things, because they're all symptoms of a larger organizational bias. The workplace was designed with men in mind, and women can't be part of that design until the seemingly small things are brought to light.

Up until the 1970s, women made up a small fraction of major orchestras like the New York Philharmonic: fewer than 5% of the musicians were women. Auditions back then were all face-to-face. There was a concern that a bias existed—not for men, but for students who came from certain conservatories or had certain backgrounds. In an effort to test for and remove this bias, major orchestras across the country began conducting blind auditions in the mid-seventies. The candidate is seated behind a screen and plays their entire audition for the judges unseen; no words are spoken, and the judging sheets use a randomly assigned candidate number rather than the candidate's name.

What was found immediately through the initial rounds of blind auditions was that there *was* an unconscious bias, but not just for schooling or background as was initially assumed. The number of women in the orchestra jumped immediately from 5 percent to 10 percent by 1980 and continued to climb rapidly as new hires were made. By 1997, the percentage was 25 percent, and today it's a nearly fifty-fifty male to female ratio. When asked up front, no judge would admit to marking a female candidate lower than a male candidate, but the evidence was incontrovertible. These biases exist, and they must be acknowledged for change to occur.

Although unconscious bias is a big part of the issue, and something the authors aim to bring awareness to, both of them have experienced explicit coaching to play down their "female-ness" in order to hew to the status quo. Bonnie assimilated to wear blue and black suits, white buttondowns, and light makeup. She's been coached specifically to fade into the background—to not stand out. It took a long time, but she finally got to a point about 10 years ago when she decided she'd dress however she wanted. Since the change, she's had younger colleagues tell her that it's nice to see a woman at a high level in the company who "dresses like a woman." Beyond the pride of being a role model for these younger women, it struck Bonnie that the only reason her own feminine dress and traits would stick out to the younger set is if they'd never seen it modeled before at the senior leadership level. Similarly, Jessica has been told not to wear makeup and heels, no dresses, no jewelry, ensure her clothes are not formfitting, and to pull back her longer hair. Essentially, she's been told to look less female.

Jessica's response to those suggestions tends to err on the side of wearing taller heels.

### DEBUNKING MYTHS

Before getting too far into the meat of this book, it's important to address a few of the ever-present myths in the discussion about gender inclusion.

## MYTH 1: THE PLAYING FIELD IS LEVEL; WOMEN NEED TO STEP UP TO THE PLATE

This is an easy myth to debunk, yet it remains one of the most pervasive. Put simply: the playing field is not, and has never been, level.

Organizational culture wasn't created with women in mind. The workforce, historically, has been male dominated: the office was associated with males, and the home was associated with females. The work environment, therefore, naturally designed itself around the needs, preferences, and lifestyles of men. No one came up with a nefarious plan to specifically *exclude* women, but because women weren't there, they were never taken into consideration.

This design bias extends to just about every little aspect of workplace life there is. Everything is designed for men. Take the timing of meetings, for instance. Have you ever known a mother who left work to pick her kids up from school, drop them at sports practice, and scrambled to make it back in time for a 4 p.m. meeting that just as easily could have been scheduled at 11 a.m.? Also consider the temperature of the office—as low as 68 degrees! This setting comes from a thermal comfort formula based on male metabolism established back in the 1960s. You don't even have to dive into giant issues like maternity leave to find the bias; it's as clear as day when you see women bringing blankets and space heaters to their desks.

As a society, with all the advancements we've made, the inherent dichotomy of *Man = Work* and *Woman = Home* is embedded deeply within our beliefs, behaviors, policies, and procedures. The issue is not to learn, but rather to *unlearn* in order to change these deeply embedded beliefs. We're not going to create a complete paradigm shift, but we can certainly agree that the myth of a level playing field is just that—a myth. And it's a myth that not only permeates the conversation, but one that has pushed many women to opt out of leadership or the workplace altogether.

## MYTH 2: ON AN UNEVEN PLAYING FIELD, IT'S UP TO WOMEN TO FIT IN

If you Google the term "gender diversity," you'll get hundreds of thousands of hits. Nearly all of it is advice on how to assimilate, aimed at women: *Be more confident. Be assertive. Ask for what you're worth. Dress professionally* (this usually means in neutral colors, boxy lines, and without any classically feminine touches like hairstyles and makeup). Some of the hits will also be for leadership seminars that are meant to "help women help themselves." Our society dictates that professional women be well groomed and look put-together. Research tells us that looking put-together, or as some would call it, "having executive presence," is key to a woman being successful and getting ahead in business. According to the Center for Talent Innovation, it may not be the most important factor, but it's "table stakes." While only 5 percent of leaders consider appearance a key factor in executive presence, 83 percent say unkempt attire detracts from a woman's executive presence.

Much of the "help" out there is a complete effort to fix women. While it obviously serves a purpose—that many search results don't lie—if we dig ourselves deeper into the trench of believing that the onus is on women to create the change, then in 20 years, we'll be standing around wondering why we still haven't made progress.

Those with the right advice can help women work more assertively, help them to network smarter, and help them to advocate for themselves. However, if the core culture of the workplace doesn't change, then all of that effort will eventually go to waste. Women will remain frustrated, trying to wedge themselves into a system that was not designed with them in mind. As Gloria Steinem said, "Don't think about making *women* fit the world—think about making the world fit *women.*"

## MYTH 3: PROGRESS FOR WOMEN DIMINISHES STATUS AND OPPORTUNITY FOR MEN

Many women have attended conferences on women in leadership. Most of the time, the agenda is dominated by women speaking to women. There are sometimes men in the audience, men who have a vested interest in making the workforce more equal and inclusive; however, they often sit silently. The authors aren't surprised. So much of what's out there on this topic takes a stance *against* men, as though the only way to make the point that women need to be included is to bash the other side. Men have the motivation to join the conversation, but at the same time, they simply don't want to be attacked for saying the wrong thing. They don't know the right thing to say, and there's no room to figure that out without causing offense. They don't want to speak up only to be misinterpreted.

Gender inclusion goes both ways, because this can't be a conversation solely between women. Drawing men into the conversation means empowering them to say the right thing from the outset, to test their opinions and raise awareness of their biases, and to let them know what to do when they *do* make mistakes.

Bonnie has been able to conduct her own experiments on how to get this conversation started. She's held open discussion sessions where men and women can hash out the common disconnect between "he *said*" and "she *heard*." She's witnessed incredible aha moments that otherwise wouldn't have happened because people feel awkward or afraid of offending their coworkers. She's seen that given the chance to be vulnerable in a place where they know they're not going to get bashed, men not only recognize their blind spots, but they actively want to improve, they want to join the conversation, and they want to help out. They're often just too afraid of foot-in-mouth syndrome, so they stay quiet.

Arguably an even more important concern that men have is the view that progress for women means fewer opportunities for men—in essence that it is a zero-sum game. The research, which will be shared in chapter 1, clearly demonstrates that gender diversity creates more opportunities for everyone—not just women! It is definitely *not* a zero-sum game. Recognition needs to be given to the benefit of having more diverse thought at the table, even if more thinkers are wearing heels.

### MYTH 4: GENDER EXCLUSION IS A WOMAN'S ISSUE

Women naturally lead the gender inclusion conversation because they're the ones being affected by a male-designed work environment. But men are the ones in senior leadership positions; men hold the majority of the positions of power. The conversation, therefore, is largely in vain if we can't get men involved—not involved in the sense that they're being talked *at*, but involved at a deeper level, where they can participate in ideas and actions that will bring about the necessary change. Jessica recalls the number of times that she has invited men, her own male team members, to join women's employee resource group events or other conferences, only to be told that it was a "women's group" or a "women's thing."

Over the past 20 years, there's definitely been an improvement across the board. Language, for one, is much more inclusive, and you don't hear as much of the female objectification or sexist language so pervasive decades ago, at least in the United States. There's also an overall awareness of the *need* for inclusiveness, even if the basic framework of the gender gap is still in place. But simply the lack of outrageousness, and the presence of awareness, isn't enough to drill down deep into the unconscious bias that exists. Our brains are lazy, and they automatically look for patterns based on previous input. We make decisions and assessments about people without consciously thinking about it. Men are in more positions of power because *that's what we're used to*. Our brains have created bias toward men in these roles.

Another reason men need to be involved in the conversation

is that women are afraid to be the only ones sticking their necks out for women. When they're the only ones speaking up, it becomes a "women's issue." The conversation loses relevance and shifts from a conversation about *all* of us to a conversation about only *some* of us. This conversation *is* about all of us—women and men. Addressing gender bias, and making space for gender inclusion, is the joint responsibility of the men and women who share the work environment.

## MYTH 5: WOMEN ARE WOMEN'S WORST ENEMIES

This myth is possibly the most harmful: that a woman's worst enemy at work is another woman. How many times have you heard women described as "catty," or heard people shrug knowingly when two women have a disagreement? It's easy to paint a narrative that the only thing holding women back is their jealousy and inability to connect with their own gender.

For the authors, this myth is the most ridiculous and easily disproven of all. First of all, just from their own experience at work, it's obviously false; look inside any corporation, and you'll see a full roster of women-in-leadership sessions, female mentoring programs, and women-focused conferences. There's a clear push of support from women to women. The reason this myth is so harmful is that it narrows the female focus down to one nasty trait: jealousy. It allows a picture to be painted of female motivation, one that women have been battling throughout known history. It makes it easy to dismiss our efforts, and gives people an easy out on confronting their bias. *Of course women can't get ahead in the workplace,* the thinking goes. *They can't stop sabotaging each other.*

Sheryl Sandberg and Adam Grant wrote a series of essays together for the *Sunday Times,* wherein they examined the specific experiences of women in the workplace. They dismantled the catty-woman myth—they showed that women are actually the primary drivers of opportunities for other women and that women in leadership positions actively seek to bring more women up to their level. Their research proved, and the authors feel strongly, that, more often than not, women pay it forward for other women.

## WE ALL RISE TOGETHER

The intention of this book is to *(un)skirt the issues* creating and perpetuating bias in the workplace. The authors aim to bring to light some of the most common pitfalls in male-oriented dialogue and behavior within the workplace, and to provide simple practices for men looking to improve their interactions and gender inclusiveness. The intention is to equip the Well-Intentioned Man to better handle those daily, sticky situations, and to give them practical advice and motivation to join in the advocacy for a truly inclusive work environment.

Teams are more functional, productive, and effective when the widest landscape of views and ideas are taken into account. A perspective other than the status quo—male, white, balding, and middle-aged—in the workforce will advance business and cultural development further than the status quo ever could. Human progress is set on a timeline of inclusion; the more we've become connected across cultures, geographies, and identities, the further we've advanced in every field you can think of. Gender inclusion is no different, and with this book, Bonnie and Jessica hope to give men the knowledge and confidence that they need to model and to advocate for gender inclusion across industries and throughout the working world.

# CHAPTER ONE

# Just the Facts, Ma'am

—

## NUMBERS DON'T LIE

Women constitute more than half of the population of the globe, but most are not reaching top positions in any of the world's professions. In the corporate sector globally, women make up 15 percent of C-suite executive or board positions. In the United States, only 4.8 percent of the CEOs of Fortune 500 companies are women; worldwide, women hold just 3.4 percent of CEO positions. Beyond for-profit leadership, women only make up 20 percent of the top echelons of the US nonprofit sector. Furthermore, of the world's 199 heads of state, only 9 are women, and men still constitute 87 percent of positions in parliaments globally. However, the economics of supply and demand favor women's career advancement, though the reality doesn't reflect this yet. Women have higher college graduation rates and earn more degrees (including MBAs) than men, but they remain underrepresented in nearly every level of organizations: CEOs (4 percent), executive officers (14 percent), board of directors (19 percent), and mid-level management (37 percent). This means that companies forego the positive business impact of greater female representation, which includes higher rates of return, more effective risk management, and better organizational performance.

In 2015, the *New York Times* reported fewer large companies are run by women than by men named "John." Similarly, on an analysis done by accounting firm EY, the firm found that there are more men named John, Robert, William, and James on S&P 1500 boards than *all women* on boards combined.

Women aren't reaching senior-leadership levels for two reasons: they're dropping out of the executive track before they get there (intentionally or unintentionally) or opting out of the workforce entirely. A Gallup study showed that the United States used to have one of the world's highest labor-force participation rates among women between the ages of 25 and 54; now it has one of the lowest. According to the Bureau of Labor statistics, women in the workplace grew significantly from 1975 to 2000 to a peak at 59.9 percent women aged 16 and older in the workforce. Since the turn of the century, it has continued to decline—58.6 percent in 2010 and 56.7 percent by the end of 2015.

A 2015 study by *Lean In* and McKinsey & Co. found that the barriers to advancement for women are numerous. Women get less face time with bosses and senior colleagues than their male colleagues, for example, and that gap widens as both genders advance up the ladder. For some women, during their thirties, they choose to begin their "family journey." This is often once they've proven that they're competent at their jobs—and when networking becomes more important. This is the time when being a part of the guys' network is one of the reasons that men excel past women in the workplace. Men go to happy hours and golf events, which means that they also learn about job opportunities that most women will not hear about; they meet with the decision makers, and they simply get to know more people. Showing up counts at this point in their careers, but it is impractical for many women to accomplish.

Forty-eight percent of the US labor force is women—with 7 out of 10 of those women ages 25 to 54. Fifty-eight percent of working mothers have children under the age of three years old. In addition, most employed women work full time and year round. However, a wage gap persists. The World Economic Forum's 2016 Global Gender Gap report found that the United States ranks 45th out of 49 other countries when it comes to creating income parity between genders.

One of the conclusions from the report is that the United States' ranking, sharply lower than the year before, is due in part to an overall decline in women's workforce participation. A decline in overall participation means a decline in women in senior leadership positions. The data confirms that women are not reaching top levels, and many are opting out altogether.

On a more positive note, a World Economic Forum study showed the United States closed the education gender gap significantly in 2016. What this means is that although fewer women are working, the country still possesses a huge pool of educated female talent. Now, we need to remove the obstacles to allow them to advance.

To date, most efforts to eradicate gender bias in the workplace have been—however well-intentioned—almost entirely about "fixing" women. Clearly, the common belief is still that women are their own worst enemies and that their lack of confidence must be a key barrier to advancement. This is confirmed by a 2014 Harvard Business Review study citing that women hold back from climbing the work ladder until they feel 100 percent ready for an opportunity. On the other hand, their male counterparts raise their hand even before they are more than 60 percent qualified because they are confident that they'll learn what they need to learn along the way. So, confidence is an issue, but there's more to the story.

Statistics show that despite collective efforts—despite all of the coaching, literature, employee resource organizations, and networking groups, women haven't advanced to the levels that they seek and they are opting out of the workplace at record numbers. Meanwhile, workplaces need gender balance to truly excel and remain competitive. The "fix women" lens has become more and more frustrating for the countless women who don't believe they need to be fixed. They've leaned in—way in—and they've sat at the table, yet they're still hitting roadblocks. What women and companies need is for men to engage in examining the unconscious biases that exist in the workplace and to become advocates and allies for women. The majority of decision makers in the workplace are still men, and without their active participation, the workplace will not change.

Ashton Kutcher's example illustrates the effect of men engaging to make a difference. Oftentimes, when men speak up, public response is quicker, policies are enacted to address them faster, and products go to market to solve them sooner than when women speak up. Ashton Kutcher, the model-turned-actor, lamented the scarcity of changing tables in men's public restrooms after becoming a father, urging his fans to #BeTheChange on his Facebook page. Within days, Kutcher received 245,266 likes, 14,065 shares, and a plethora of comments. He created a petition to further his position, stating, "It is 2015, families are diverse, and it is an injustice to assume that it's only a woman's job to handle changing diapers. This assumption is gender stereotyping and companies should be supporting all parents that shop at their stores equally—no matter their gender." The campaign was a slam dunk when both Costco and Target dedicated themselves to the implementation of family-friendly restrooms in their stores. Would the same response have been given—and so swiftly—to a female celebrity?

At one time, Bonnie was guilty of not realizing that women weren't necessarily the ones who needed fixing. Ten years ago, she spoke to a group of women about climbing the corporate ladder. The title of Bonnie's presentation was "There Are No Glass Ceilings, Only Sticky Floors." The talk was about all the things women do to hold themselves back. At that point in her career, Bonnie was convinced that women weren't advancing because of factors they could control, like how they carried themselves, for example, or a lack of willingness to speak up at meetings. Over time, she realized that behavioral changes and confidence weren't enough. More change was needed, and most of it was beyond the control of the women she was trying to help.

Let's be clear, gender exclusion is not caused by any one thing that women, men, or organizations say, do, or think. The roadblocks are more holistic: when the organizational culture of the workplace was designed, it wasn't designed with women in mind. It's a simple concept, one that is easy to overlook, because it affects every aspect of work and personal life. If work hours fit school hours, women would not be missing critical meetings because their kids need to be picked up. There are also challenges for women without children. If workplaces demonstrated flexibility and offered concierge services, women (who still are responsible for most of the household activities) would benefit greatly from a work-life integration perspective, and so would men! Most of our workplaces have been run the same way for so long that we don't even realize how unfriendly they can be for women.

Unconscious bias is rooted in the very way our brains work. The primitive parts of our brain are designed to ensure survival and conserve energy by looking for patterns and shortcuts. In this vein, perhaps men, without even realizing it, select, reward, and promote leaders based on what is familiar and comfortable to them: people similar to themselves. In the 2016 US presidential election, Donald Trump made the comment that Hillary Clinton didn't look very presidential. Well, of course she didn't; there's never been a female president.

A popular Twitter feed, intended to highlight biased things often said to women in the workplace, @manwhohasitall, pinpoints our unconscious gender bias best with this satire: "Men, if you speak up in a meeting and want to be taken seriously, dress smart, but not too smart. Stay calm and avoid appearing too ambitious"—said no one, ever, at least not to a man.

## THE IMPACT OF WOMEN IN THE WORKPLACE

There's an important reason why future-thinking companies put gender inclusion at the top of their culture priorities: gender-diverse businesses are proven to be more competitive and bring in more revenue. Women in the workplace drive progress and success. Companies that have a fifty-fifty gender split in senior operating roles show, on average, a 19 percent higher return on equity (ROE) than companies with fewer women at the top. In profitable companies, a move from 0 percent to 30 percent female leaders correlates with a 15 percent increase in a net revenue margin. And, perhaps most telling, the most gender-diverse companies are 15 percent more likely to show overall financial returns higher than their industry means.[1]

A Gallup study shows that gender-diverse teams not only perform better, but they also provide a greater economic

---

1   https://www.paradigm4parity.com/problem#the-facts

benefit to their companies. Gender diversity has another, bigger impact that is less often recognized: it helps men to step outside of traditional roles and follow their unique talents. This is important because men also still face challenges when they attempt to pursue roles outside of the norm. When one of Bonnie's sons got out of the military service, he wanted to be a nurse. But his friends and brothers teased him so much about becoming a "male nurse" that he eventually switched his degree program to become an emergency medical technician. Good news, though: he has switched his major back to nursing, so he will be a nurse—not a "male nurse."

Stereotypical roles hamper everyone. Keeping women in boxes keeps men in boxes too. More women in the workplace will help both genders to break out of their respective boxes.

Policies designed to create better work-life effectiveness have been and still are generally considered beneficial primarily to mothers. However, companies are finding that everyone ends up gaining from such policies. Recently, Bonnie held open discussions among employees about potential concerns over women in leadership. Several men in management-level positions expressed their satisfaction over the ability to have flexible work schedules as a result of new initiatives that were primarily thought to be for women. They also said they'd love the opportunity to work part time and have benefits. Men are juggling work and family too, and they are also seeking more balance at every opportunity.

Jessica offers an example that she encountered when a company created an internal sales team that leveraged technology (the phone and e-mail) to sell in a more cost-effective way. The new sales jobs carried a great deal of flexibility, and applicants were originally envisioned to be stay-at-home moms or working moms that could not travel frequently, as other salespeople do. But this particular sales force now includes stay-at-home dads and single women who don't want to go into the office every day for a variety of reasons, some as simple as commute time. In the twenty-first century, give men and women control over where and how they work, whenever possible. Creating culture change so that working flexibly is embraced and not an underused and overhyped benefit is desired by all employees.

When it comes to sons, a study by Harvard Business School Professor Kathleen McGinn found that young boys who grow up with a working mother have a greater appreciation for women in the workforce. A large percentage of these boys end up marrying someone who works outside the home as well. McGinn has said, "There is no single policy or practice that can eliminate gender gaps at work and at home. But being raised by a working mother appears to come very close to that. Women raised by a working mother do better in the workplace, and men raised by a working mother contribute more at home."

If the benefits mentioned above are not compelling enough, the economic benefits of increased gender equity and flexibility in the norms, policies, and practices at companies are extraordinary. For example, research from KPMG, commissioned by Vodaphone, shows that 16 weeks of parental leave actually saves companies $19 billion a year. It does this primarily by saving companies the cost of finding and hiring employees to take the jobs of those who leave after having a baby. Additional compelling research by McKinsey shows that if gender equality in the workplace is achieved by 2025, the Gross Domestic Product (GDP) would grow globally by $28 trillion. In the U.S., that would be 11 percent GDP growth and in developing countries, the numbers go even higher.

**HOW TO KEEP A GOOD WOMAN**

A work environment that prioritizes gender inclusion and strives to meet the different needs of employees not only attracts top talent, but also retains that talent. Recruiting at the best universities in the United States and abroad doesn't matter if those hired don't want to stay. Companies that are conscious about controlling costs, which are most, would be better off directing recruiting dollars toward improving employee culture to keep the people that they have and to attract the ones they want.

Every company faces the challenge of employee retention. People point to millennials as the driving force behind the move to shape workplace culture to fit employee needs, but the truth is that workers across a wide age range are in need of and advocating for change. In many companies, senior leadership is starting to realize that in order to attract high-potential women and men, they must transform the workplace culture to fit their needs.

The culture gap is the difference between the current workplace culture and the culture preferred by existing and potential employees, and its impact cannot be underestimated. When the culture gap is wide, 44 percent of women are likely to leave an employer compared to 46 percent of men, figures that are roughly equal. Neither group wants to stay in an uncomfortable culture. But when the culture gap is narrow, only 3 percent of women are likely to leave compared to 23 percent of men.

What this shows is that while the culture gap is important to both genders, women, more than men, will stay at a company whose culture is aligned with what they want and need. A narrow culture gap engenders a greater level of company loyalty from women.

In addition, a narrow culture gap builds engagement for everyone. The more excited people are to go to work every day, the more likely they are to commit to the long haul, and weathering bumps in the road is easier. Also, employee engagement is infectious and creates a ripple effect across company culture and drives business results.

While a common belief exists that pay is the number one reason people stay (or leave) with an employer, the research paints a different picture. Studies show that pay is not at the top of the list. Feeling valued, included, and listened to are much bigger priorities. Having a strong sense of purpose and believing that the company is invested in employees and that there is an ability to grow and develop are also higher up on the list than pay. Without these factors, both women and men are more likely to leave.

Out of 300,000 people polled in a 2016 Gallup study, 48 percent of the women said they were either actively looking or actively watching for another job opportunity. An outdated company culture affecting women both personally and professionally was a top reason cited. The World Economic Forum found a strong correlation between a company's competitiveness and how it educates and uses female talent.

If a narrow culture gap keeps women at a company, how do you close that gap when it's a yawning chasm?

## HARMFUL EFFECTS OF UNCONSCIOUS BIAS FOR WOMEN

A well-known study demonstrates the power of the unconscious bias that we all possess as a society. While teaching a class on gender perceptions at Columbia University, Stanford professor Frank Flynn gave students a case study about an extremely successful Silicon Valley entrepreneur (real life, venture capitalist Heidi Roizen). Half the students were told the entrepreneur's name was Howard; the other half were told the name was Heidi. When the students were asked to give their impressions of the entrepreneur, those who thought it was Heidi deemed her selfish and aggressive. Not so with Howard, who was deemed likeable and competent.

There is another pervasive assumption that all women want to become mothers. The assumption carries the baggage that women must then figure out how to balance family and career, and that the latter will suffer. Here's the thing: not every woman wants children. And, if she does, her employer should not automatically assume that a desire for flexibility must be a burden to the company. When an employer interviews a man for a potential job, no one ever takes into consideration whether his desire for a family will conflict with his job down the road, even though men become fathers just as often as women become mothers.

Men often have the best of intentions, but they end up misreading women in the workplace. How many times have you noticed a woman taking a strong and impassioned stance on an issue, only to be told (or to think yourself) that she's "being emotional"? The discussion will continue, women are told, after they've cooled down—when in fact they were simply stating a position. Jessica is quick to point to examples when she has seen women bring facts and data to a discussion on a topic they believe in with conviction and passion, only to be cast aside as though they were wearing their heart on their sleeve. Why can't the facts and data speak for themselves when coming from a woman? Why must we first assess her emotional state? Chapter 10 will dive into this very question.

Research, books, and articles on gender bias routinely suggest that men need to understand how women think. They stress that men need to know what it's like to walk in women's heels. But do they?

The authors believe that a better and more efficient route would be to help men understand and recognize their unconscious biases, and to provide guidance on how to manage them. Expecting men to be able to dive deep into the female psyche isn't entirely realistic, nor is the reverse (women understanding the male psyche). But expecting them to understand that men and women are different, and to be more open and inclusive, is realistic and doable.

A key aspect to this approach is practice. Rather than trying to figure out women, men can ask themselves in any given situation whether they would ask a male colleague the same question they plan to pose to a female colleague. If the answer is no, don't ask that question. For example, would a male boss request that a male colleague get coffee for everyone at a meeting? Would he ask a male subordinate with a wife and four children how he "does it all?" During a job interview, would he ask a male applicant if he's discussed the time commitments of the position with his wife?

The Man Who Has It All tweeter highlighted this approach when he asked, "Is fatherhood the end for career men?"

At this point, you may be shaking your head in disbelief that these questions have been seriously addressed to women. They have—time and time again! So, hold on to your seat—there's more to come, along with guidance on how to improve the conversation.

## THE WELL-INTENTIONED MAN (WIM)

The easy response to these problems is to cast blame unilaterally on men and to demonize them as a monolithic group. This isn't helpful. This is the *opposite* of helpful. The real truth is that workplaces are full of men who want to understand women, to support them, and to see them excel. Jessica and Bonnie call such a boss or colleague a Well-Intentioned Man (WIM).

The traits that define a WIM will be detailed in chapter 2, but in brief, WIMs are interested and even eager to make their unconscious biases conscious. They bounce e-mails off female colleagues to ensure that their communication is inclusive. They run ideas past the women who will be affected by them to make sure there are no gaps in inclusion that they may have missed. They are open to learning from a different vantage point. They ask for feedback. They sincerely want to change but don't know how. They need a guide. That's why this book was written.

A man often wakes up to gender bias after he marries a woman, and especially when he has a daughter. Wharton School professor, Adam Grant, described this phenomenon well in a 2013 *New York Times* op-ed entitled "Why Men Need Women." Grant writes:

> When Bill Gates was on his way to becoming the world's

richest man, he rejected advice to set up a charitable foundation…but changed his mind the following year. Just three years later, Gates ranked third on Fortune's list of the most generous philanthropists in America. In between, he welcomed his first child: a daughter.

In the workplace, gender inclusiveness has a direct economic benefit. Grant cites research that analyzes the approximate payoff between 1992 and 2006 for 1,500 S&P companies after they put women in top leadership positions. It was more than $40 million. "Increases in motivation, cooperation, and innovation in companies," Grant writes, "may be fueled not only by the direct actions of female leaders, but also by their influence on male leaders."

A WIM has the desire to be the best leader possible. Jessica once mentioned to a longtime friend, now the CEO of a petrochemical company, that 3:30 p.m. meetings were fatal for many female employees because moms wanted to be there for their kids when they got off the school bus or needed to be picked up from school.

A light bulb went off for the CEO. "I'd never thought of that," he said.

This is a man who proudly points out that having two grown, working daughters who are also moms has softened his leadership style, yet he's not embarrassed by knowledge gaps. He's open to learning and growing.

If you—one of the many WIMs in this world—are also open to learning, then this guide is designed for you! Read it, come back to it, and use it as your field guide; in doing so, you'll be on your way to fueling the change that will benefit everyone.

---

## WHAT'S THE POINT?

△ Women constitute more than half of the global population, and more women are graduating from college and with advanced degrees, yet there is a significant overall decline in women's workforce participation.

△ To date, most efforts to eradicate bias in the workplace have been focused on "fixing" women rather than leveling the playing field.

△ Gender exclusion is not caused by any one thing that women, men, or organizations do (or don't do). Rather, the obstacles are rooted in the way organizational culture was designed. It wasn't designed with women in mind.

## WHY IT MATTERS

⚠ Greater female representation in leadership is shown to have significant business impact, including higher rates of financial return, more effective risk management, better organization performance, and improved organizational climates.

⚠ Gender diversity is shown to have another, less-known effect: it helps men to step out of traditional roles and follow their unique talents and aspirations as well.

## WIMS: TIPS FOR ACTION

⚠ Give women and men control over where and how they work, whenever possible. Create culture change so that working flexibly is embraced rather than seen as an underused and over-talked-about benefit. Demonstrate flexibility in your actions as well.

⚠ Strive to reduce the culture gap to increase engagement for everyone.

⚠ Practice makes all of us better. Rather than trying to figure women out (and feigning heels), WIMs can ask themselves if they would ask a male colleague the same question they plan to ask a female. If the juxtaposed answer is no, then refrain.

# CHAPTER TWO

# So, What's a WIM to Do?

―――

As the introduction described, throughout Bonnie and Jessica's careers, they've encountered Well-Intentioned Men who are eager to help women succeed but they are not sure how to do so. Before laying out some actions that WIMs can take, let's further describe who WIMs are and what they're about.

For starters, a WIM is the antithesis of a male chauvinist: he doesn't have overt biases toward women, and he doesn't intentionally treat them poorly. He doesn't objectify or talk about them in obnoxious or distasteful ways.

A WIM is open to learning about how to create a more

inclusive environment. Often, a WIM starts examining how he can help women after he experiences a triggering event. This could be seeing a spouse experience gender adversity at work, or, like Bill Gates, it could be the birth of a daughter. When a WIM becomes an ally for a woman in the workplace, he's often a colleague or friend who is a father, grandfather, or brother to a woman.

A WIM possesses humility. He knows that he doesn't have all the answers, and he strives to recognize and eliminate unconscious bias. He'll send an e-mail to a trusted female colleague to proofread or to brainstorm with her to understand her perspective. Often, a WIM prefers that conversations take place behind closed doors because he feels slightly embarrassed or vulnerable, and he wants to ensure that he's doing the right thing.

A WIM knows that because of his gender, gut reactions as they relate to women aren't necessarily accurate or reliable. He doesn't pretend that he can know or fully understand what it's like to be a woman. He knows he has a great deal to learn. He's open-minded, and he's willing to listen and alter his approach.

A WIM isn't necessarily fully engaged in gender-diversity initiatives, but he has learned about unconscious bias and acknowledges that people often inherently gravitate toward others more like themselves. He's willing to examine his thought processes around hiring and promoting and whether they might be skewed. He intuitively knows stereotypes that permeate the workplace are often automatic and unconscious.

Finally, a WIM believes in the value of inclusion. He doesn't view the workplace from a debit/credit perspective; he doesn't believe that more women at the top means fewer men. In fact, WIMs are usually big-picture thinkers. Their view is that a more diverse and inclusive team helps the company as a whole. They know that narrowing the culture gap is essential to attracting and retaining talent of both genders.

## WHY AREN'T MORE MEN INVOLVED?

Ninety percent of the world is right-handed, and the righties don't think about what life is like for the 10 percent who are lefties. Similarly, men don't automatically spend time thinking about what it's like for a woman to operate in a work environment designed by and for men. They don't realize, for example, that often fear of failure starts at a young age for women. Research shows that girls are more likely to see failure as a sign that they are inherently deficient in some way, whereas young boys see it as a result of circumstance.

Adam Grant, the Wharton School professor mentioned in chapter 1, wrote about his own awakening in a 2015 article for *Inc.* magazine. As both an educator and organizational psychologist, Grant wrote, "I shied away from talking about gender in my Wharton classes, fearing that it would divide rather than unite." He continued, "After all, I had read overwhelming evidence that on virtually every attribute ever studied, men and women are remarkably similar—including intelligence, math, and verbal abilities."

But he changed after two female colleagues, as well as *Lean In* author Sheryl Sandberg, asked him to look at the research, analyze his own data for gender bias, and stop being silent. Grant said his naïveté was shattered. He was "mortified" at what he found, including that "men got credit for speaking up and helping, but women didn't."

Grant wrote in *Inc.* about the "chilling data" reported by *New York Times* correspondent Claire Cain Miller:

> In math, when graded anonymously, girls outperform boys, but when teachers know their names, boys do better. And when students rate their favorite professors, they describe men as "geniuses" and women as "nice."

Unfortunately, many men are hesitant and even fearful to take part in initiatives designed to advance women. The reasons include being concerned about being the target of male bashing. Men believe they might say the wrong thing and get crucified. Jessica and Bonnie have both witnessed men in the audience at women's conferences who don't utter a word.

The hesitancy of men isn't out of the ordinary. Employee resource groups designed to help gay workers rarely have straight participants, and Latino groups rarely have white members. Men believe it's not their role to join a women's group.

But this perspective creates a block for companies that want to move forward. Companies where men champion women's groups, speak at them, and listen to their ideas create a culture of transparency and openness that benefits everyone.

## THE IMPACT OF BRO TALK

Women can stop blaming men, and men can take blame off themselves, by understanding that many men aren't involved in ending bias because many simply don't understand that it is a real issue.

The real trouble comes when men who do recognize the problem are conditioned to keep quiet. They fear a loss of status among other men in the workplace and feel pressure to maintain the status quo. Former hedge fund manager, Sam Polk, described this pressure in a 2016 *New York Times* op-ed piece entitled "How Wall Street Bro Talk Keeps Women Down." As a trader on Wall Street, Polk repeatedly heard his colleagues and superiors degrade and objectify women, reducing them to body parts and sex objects.

Polk wrote, "Protesting would have violated the sanctity of the men-only space and would have risked interfering with the bonding that goes hand-in-hand with the objectification of the other sex. It would have been embarrassing and emasculating. And it would have been the end of my career." After he left Wall Street, Polk learned his wife was pregnant with a daughter.

Polk wrote, "When we dehumanize people in conversation, we give them permission to be degraded in other ways as well." Polk deeply regrets his silence in the past and calls on men in every field to insist that women be treated with respect in action and speech.

Women know this is all too common: they've been looked up and down by men, heard the catcalls, and even worse, the names used to refer to women. Women need men to speak up and shut down the bro talk.

## WHAT CAN MEN DO DIFFERENTLY?

Language that degrades women isn't always overt. Men who want to help women can eliminate subtler, objectifying language that they may use with other men—words like "sissy," "whipped," and "chick." On the surface, those words may not appear to be a big deal, but the truth is that they're divisive. Are men ever called "sweetie" or "honey" at work? We doubt it. Are men ever told that for being the first man to ever hold a certain position, they sure did a great job? As the first woman in a key role outside the United States, Jessica was praised in her evaluation for doing such a good job—for *a woman* in the role. She was surprised to see the lack of reference to her business results and employee engagement, but rather the focus on her gender.

The rule of thumb is that if you wouldn't say it to a man, you probably shouldn't say it to a woman. Don't de-emphasize an otherwise strong accolade by referencing gender.

The same thing goes for written communication. Bonnie, for example, had a performance review once in which her boss wrote that despite the time commitments that had come with becoming a grandmother, Bonnie had excelled that year. Although she was certain her boss wasn't trying to be insulting, Bonnie couldn't imagine the same thing being written about a male employee becoming a grandfather, or even being mentioned, for that matter.

The research is clear: companies perform better when more women become leaders. A man who sees himself as part of the solution, not the problem, can help to shift the entire paradigm of workplace inclusion. A rising tide lifts all boats, and diversity and inclusion is that tide. Standing with and for women creates a better workplace, and a better world, not only for men's spouses, daughters, and sisters, but for humanity.

In the next nine chapters, the authors share stories, filled with humor, strong lessons and tips for action to help (un) skirt some of these very issues.

---

## WHAT'S THE POINT?

△ Objectifying language can be subtle and pervasive: words like "sissy" and "chick," meant to imply weakness, slight women.

△ Men are conditioned not to speak up against objectifying language because they're worried that they'll be seen as violating the guy code, and not being a team player.

△ Some men are simply not aware that certain language (spoken or written) is an issue at all. It doesn't occur naturally to them. (And why would it?)

## WHY IT MATTERS

⚠ Women can't compete in a workplace where they're demeaned through language, even when that language is subtle or unintentional.

⚠ Men can't just snap their fingers and notice wording that they're not fluent in. They're not attuned to the experience of being a woman. They will not wake up one day with the epiphany without a conscious effort.

## WIMS: TIPS FOR ACTION

⚠ Acknowledge that because of your gender, your gut reactions are not always reliable or accurate, especially when it comes to women. Ask, listen, and then alter your approach where necessary.

⚠ Do not allow spoken or written bro talk to permeate the workplace.

⚠ Be conscious about using the qualifier "for a woman." Don't de-emphasize an otherwise strong accolade by referencing gender.

# CHAPTER THREE

# She's Not What You Expected

---

**WHAT HE SAID**

When Bonnie moved abroad for work, she was one of the most senior leaders in the region at that time. One night soon after she arrived, she was out at dinner and took a call from her husband, who was still back at home preparing to move the rest of their family.

After she got off the phone, an older gentleman at a nearby table asked Bonnie where she was from, noting her "beautiful American accent." Bonnie replied that she was from the United States.

"Oh, are you here for your husband's work?" the gentleman asked.

"No, I'm here for my work," Bonnie replied.

When Bonnie told the man that she was the managing director for a major product line there, his response was, "Well, you don't look like a managing director."

"What does a managing director look like?" Bonnie replied.

"Not female," he said, matter-of-factly.

Meanwhile, when Jessica was living abroad in Latin America, she too was the most senior leader in the country. Her role was broad in scope and function, and one aspect included governmental affairs responsibilities, such as meeting with the president, his staff, and the ambassador. While waiting for a meeting once in the reception area of the presidential palace, the president's photographer asked Jessica who she was there to pose with.

"Excuse me?" Jessica asked, perplexed.

Turns out, every Thursday, a different part of the constituency was featured in a photo opportunity with the president. The photographer assumed, even though Jessica was dressed in business formal attire, that she was there to model for the photo opportunity. He repeatedly apologized with a puzzled look on his face, when he learned she was there in a professional capacity for a cabinet meeting. It was clear from the look on his face that he couldn't have imagined her being there in such a capacity.

## WHAT SHE HEARD

Women frequently have experiences like the stories shared here, including a countless number of stories from the authors themselves, told best over a glass of good wine. It's unbelievably common that women are treated to opinions or assumptions about what they're *supposed* to look like. They hear that they don't look like the boss or like the person in charge. Or, if people say they did expect a woman, pejorative comments are often tacked on, "We expected someone older."

Both of the authors' reflections above are from specific experiences living outside of the United States, but we know that these experiences are not geographically restricted. Jessica recalls one of her first days as an in-house lawyer for a public company headquartered in the United States. She walked into the executive suite for a presentation to the board with her boss, the general counsel, on an acquisition target. One of the male directors bumped into Jessica, and without making eye contact, shoved a presentation at her and asked her to make a copy. Without hesitation, Jessica made the copy (although this was not her forte) and gave it to the director. She then turned, walked to the front of the board room, introduced herself and began her presentation. The director's face remained red for the entire presentation.

Assumptions not only happen in person based on preconceived notions of appearance by men, but also in other ways, and by women, as well. When one of Bonnie's male employees was trying to coordinate a meeting for her, he cc'd Bonnie on the e-mail request. The peer's female administrative assistant then contacted Bonnie directly about scheduling, assuming she was another assistant, not the boss.

### SO WHAT?

Men don't often realize that experiences and issues that aren't a big deal to them can have a very different impact for women, especially younger women. For example, Bonnie was once on an international business trip with her boss. The flight home from Italy left early in the morning, so she threw on sweat pants, put her hair up in a ponytail, and didn't apply any makeup for the trip. The flight was cancelled, and Bonnie ended up having to call her boss to catch a ride with him to another city for an alternate departure.

Bonnie was horrified that she had to drive three hours with her boss while dressed so unprofessionally. For him, it was no big deal; he wears the same casual clothes every day. But women feel constant pressure to be put together with makeup and professional clothes.

Women are taught from a young age to dress the part. They are taught that in order to be a managing director or a country manager, they must look like one. And when that look is questioned, even with subtle comments driven by unconscious bias, the effect is significant. The result is that woman are often self-conscious. Self-doubt about whether they're dressed appropriately is a common occurrence and leads to an even bigger issue—women feel that because they aren't recognized as looking the part, then they aren't deserving of it or able to live up to it either.

Along these lines, when a man looks in the mirror, he sees a *person*. When a woman looks in the mirror, she sees a *woman*. Emphasis on appearance drives the conversation away from how women actually perform in their jobs. A woman is constantly aware at work, and elsewhere, that she's operating in a man's world. No matter how high up in business or politics a woman gets, or how hard she falls, in the end, the focus is often on how she looks and dresses, not how she performs.

Research shows that nearly half of women don't feel good

about themselves unless they're wearing makeup. Women are constantly greeted with unsolicited comments on their appearance: *You look tired. You look thin. I like your outfit.* Rarely do they hear men being greeted in the same fashion—although sometimes the authors are tempted to try it just to see the reaction! Have you ever heard anyone greet a man by telling him he looks tired? Women, especially if they happened not to put on under-eye concealer that day, hear it constantly.

The most crippling aspect of this phenomenon is that a persistent emphasis on appearance plays into stereotypes about what an executive should look like or how an employee in a particular role should behave, and women are conditioned to follow along. Stereotypes result in self-handicapping behavior for women.

One of the ways Jessica intentionally combats stereotypes in her leadership position is to dress to express her femininity. When appropriate, Jessica wears dresses, makeup, and sometimes even heels (although, as a runner, she prefers flats). The feedback she receives from women, both younger and older, is that they appreciate her not trying to disguise who she is—as a woman. In addition, as Jessica has developed as a leader, and her confidence and brand has grown, she's even started doing the opposite: stopping in the office after the gym (in her gym clothes) or changing into Pilates clothes at the office for a lunch-time session. Jessica is making the intentional showing to her organization that not only is she a female leader in dresses, but she's also a normal person that doesn't always look put together. In doing so, she continues to shake up stereotypes about what a senior leader should look like.

*Miss Representation*, the 2011 documentary produced by Jennifer Siebel Newsom, provides powerful examples of how women are exhaustively stereotyped through the lens of a culture dominated by men. The result is under-representation for girls and women of what females in top positions should look like. Says Siebel Newsom:

> The media sells the idea that for girls and women, their value lies in youth, beauty, and sexuality, not in their capacity as leaders. Boys learn that their success is tied to dominance, power, and aggression.

Jessica attended a women's leadership acceleration conference that included a panel by a firm that coaches executives. The firm executive that spoke said the critique most often given to women is that they don't have "executive presence." Such an opaque evaluation plays into stereotypes and leaves unanswered questions: **What does that mean? Does executive presence mean a certain age? Hair length? Style? Outfit? What?**

Jessica's father, a retired executive, also received comments as he was climbing the ladder that he didn't look "executive enough." Sometimes he'd wear baseball caps to work and forget to take them off. Other times, his tie was crooked. And it was the tie that his kids bought him. Yet even with that feedback and coaching, in the end, her father scaled the ladder. Would it have been the same result if he were instead a woman? Specifically, research from the Center for Talent Innovation shows that women have a smaller window of executive presence acceptability than men. Many of the missteps that can throw off a woman's executive presence are not only unique to women, but are also easier to make—and harder to recover from, especially with regard to appearance. According to 42 percent of survey respondents, unkempt nails detract from a woman's executive presence. At the same time, 37 percent say "overly done" nails are un-leaderlike. Similar contradictions arose from focus group participants, who stated that too much make-up undermined a woman's credibility—but then faulted women for looking too frumpy or unpolished.

Our society's preoccupation with a woman's appearance creates a tightrope for a female in the workplace and especially in work-related social settings. She repeatedly finds herself in stressful situations that a man would never encounter. For example, Jessica attends various advisory groups and sales meetings each year. Business meetings usually occur for half the day, while the other half of the day is consumed with social events, often including spouses of her male colleagues. Not surprisingly, many of these meetings are in destination spots, and the social events are often centered around the beach: swimming, sailing, snorkeling, and the like.

For Jessica, these conferences are often a lose-lose predicament. As a woman, if she wears a swimsuit at such events, she's concerned that she will be viewed as flaunting her body in front of male colleagues, and even worse, their spouses, or she will create an awful mental image for years to come. If she doesn't put on a swimsuit at all, she can't participate, and is deemed aloof or cold, not a team player. After much consternation and heartburn, at the most recent event, Jessica settled on wearing a discreet one-piece with cover-up pants, while quasi-participating in the activities.

Jessica's male colleagues were clueless about her stress level over the issue. When she finally mentioned it as the team was discussing the next agenda, some of her male colleagues were dismissive. She was told that the matter wasn't a big deal. At no time did she receive feedback that they hadn't considered the problem because it never affects them.

While it may seem like an obvious action for Jessica in both instances to simply wear a modest one-piece by itself, the issue is so fraught with peril that she didn't want to risk it. She feared, and still does, in career potential discussions, that the vision (good or bad) that permeated was of her in a swimsuit rather than her 10-year career plan. The truth is that Jessica couldn't win, no matter what she chose to do in that scenario. What does this indicate? That the scenario has to change.

**PUT IN PRACTICE**

By becoming more aware of the pressure women face over their appearance (some of which is admittedly self-inflicted from a young age), men can help to create more inclusion in the workplace. For example, a WIM could vote down a proposal to hold a team-building exercise at the beach or on a sailboat. Men need to realize how agonizing it is for most women to dress for events that include their colleagues' spouses, nonetheless put them in a swimsuit. This simple action is a conscious one, recognizing the deep cultural conditioning over appearance in our society that women face on a regular basis.

Men can also pay attention to the compliments and comments they make to their female colleagues and subordinates. When conversations begin or focus on women's appearance, it automatically detracts from her substance. By working to shift his own focus away from physical appearance, a WIM helps to shift a company away from being a place where a woman is objectified or judged solely based on appearance to a more gender-inclusive environment.

When men make these small, conscious decisions and actions, huge changes open up for women in the workplace by forcing organizations to focus on the substance that women have to offer.

And for the women who are reading this book (and who probably bought it for the WIMs in their life), speak up. Rather than lose sleep over whether to wear a swimsuit, speak up and let your voice be heard.

Organizations should create the space that allows for these discussions. Getting closer to more gender inclusion means taking into consideration what a gender-neutral or mixed-gender- appropriate activity might include. It should also encourage organizations to consider increasing the number of women in certain roles so that it is not so extraordinary that there is a woman managing director or country manager. Having more women visible in these organizations will begin to change the conversation and attack the unconscious bias.

## WHAT'S THE POINT?

△ Women are frequently reminded, implicitly or explicitly, that they do not fit the so-called traditional leader mold. Assumptions not only happen in-person based on preconceived notions of appearance by men, but also in other ways as well, and even by women.

△ Too much focus is placed on female appearance and dress rather than performance and substance. Men aren't greeted with comments about their appearance, ever. When's the last time you heard someone tell a man, "You look tired," or, "I love your outfit"?

△ When a man looks in the mirror, he sees a person. When a woman looks in the mirror, she sees a woman. Women are constantly aware that they are operating in a man's world at work.

## WHY IT MATTERS

△ Subtle and not-so-subtle biases in the workplace position women at a disadvantage.

△ These biases define executive presence for women in a way that is replete with inconsistencies for women.

△ Women feel that because they aren't recognized as looking the part, or because they are questioned regarding their appearance, that they are not deserving and that they cannot live up to the role either.

## WIMS: TIPS FOR ACTION

△ Be mindful about whether work activities (or social events with colleagues) are gender friendly—or gender exclusive. When in doubt, ask. Women will be glad that you did, and they will probably be willing to provide you with honest feedback.

△ Pay attention to how many times in a given week that you comment about a woman's appearance or dress at work (versus the number of times you comment about a man's).

△ Be a role model for inclusiveness by avoiding references to appearance or dress, and actively model referencing performance, behavior, and contributions instead. Lead the organization to focus on the substance that women have to offer.

# CHAPTER FOUR

# She Doesn't Want a Free Ride

---

## WHAT HE SAID

Not long ago, Bonnie initiated conversations with the men in her organization, persuading them of the importance of an initiative aimed at helping more women advance to leadership positions. She wanted to understand their concerns. A senior male leader told her that he was still trying to wrap his head around why the company had created specific targets for the initiative aimed at women, instead of diversity more broadly.

Bonnie explained to him that inclusion was going to help the company become stronger as a result of more diverse perspectives, and that, since 50 percent of the world's population are women, gender inclusion is important for the company's long-term competitiveness. Toward the end of the conversation, she stressed that the goal was to create more opportunities for everyone, not just women.

As they finished up, the male leader said, "Okay. I'm more comfortable, and I accept it, as long as women don't think that they're going to get a free ride."

Bonnie had to stop her jaw from hitting the table. She took a few moments to gather herself, then calmly asked, "So, are you admitting that you've had a free ride for the last twenty years, then? Men, by definition, have had most of the opportunities. Now we're saying that we want to level the playing field and give women more opportunities. Your comment would imply that you think you've had a free ride all these years."

It was like a light bulb went off for her colleague. He realized the implications of what he'd said immediately.

For Bonnie, his comment was educational: it showed her that many men look at gender inclusion efforts as a potential threat. Here's the truth: there's not a woman that either of the authors has encountered in the workplace who wants a free ride. In fact, most women say, "I never want to get a job because I'm a woman. I want to get a job because I'm capable, and I *happen to be* a woman."

At one of Jessica's previous employers, meetings intentionally weren't held before 8 a.m. or after 3 p.m. Most people assumed that this practice was to allow for a flexible start and end to the day. Some may have even thought it was so that moms could take their kids to school or pick them up (and they certainly did). When Jessica learned about people's assumptions, however, she vocalized that the timing wasn't just for moms, but it was for anyone who wanted flexibility, such as a dad who wanted to coach sports after school, or for her to take a 6 a.m. spin class and then go home and shower before work. She had to change the assumption that the initiative was designed to give women special treatment, and turn the conversation into one about what was beneficial for everyone.

**WHAT SHE HEARD**

In many companies, the words "flexibility" and "accommodation" when it comes to policies are often considered code for efforts to help women specifically. Yet women don't want to be the exception in any workplace circumstance. Again, they don't want a free ride, or even the appearance of one. For example, women are afraid of not being seen as high-level performers if they work from home while men don't. A woman may not be considered capable of a promotion to a high-responsibility position if her availability is questioned. This happens more than women would like to admit.

Bonnie, for example, attended a leadership conference where a senior executive told his male colleagues that he understands that women need more flexibility, and potentially, a lighter travel schedule. But he was going to hold his male colleagues to the same standards he endured as he rose through the ranks: heavy travel and long hours.

Men often fail to understand that well-intentioned support that applies only to women only can actually hurt women at work. Women don't want to be special, and they repeatedly make this very clear, but they're not always heard. It's similar to when native English speakers try to communicate with non-English speakers: sometimes they just get louder and louder when repeating words that the other person doesn't understand. The problem isn't that the non-English speaker can't hear them, however, the problem is that it's not their native language. Men often don't understand that they undermine women when making gender-based exceptions because they aren't fluent in the experience of being a woman in the workplace.

Bonnie mentored a single mom who worked hard and was

an excellent employee and leader. She applied for a higher-level position and didn't get it. When she asked her boss what she could have done to better position herself for more responsibility, he told her that while she did a great job and was clearly capable, he was concerned about her ability to take on more responsibility as a single mom. The boss sincerely thought he was doing the right thing for her and for the company. He had provided her opportunities in her current position for flexibility, but those opportunities worked against her when it came time to be considered for higher levels of leadership.

Would the circumstances and outcome have been different if a single dad had applied for more responsibility?

In today's workplace, countless workers, male and female, want flexibility *and* trust. It's not a woman thing.

### SO WHAT?

Flexibility policies that only apply to women, or that appear to be gender driven, give with one hand and take away with the other. Organizations and leaders that provide them need to be aware of the unconscious biases that they perpetuate. The potential is there to hamper women from the start, creating perceptions about limited credibility and capability.

Up until now, what it means to be qualified to be an executive or leader has been defined almost entirely by men. If a company has a policy to define the kind of leadership required for a promotion, that definition was almost certainly shaped by the behavior and lifestyles of men. The deck is stacked; women are disadvantaged before they even get up to the starting gate.

Ernst & Young's global chairman and CEO, Mark Weinberger recently said, "Women don't want to be singled out and men don't want to be left out. Flexible working is NOT just a women's issue." What a great way to put it!

Other assumptions about women in the workplace abound that almost suggest that women need and should ask for exceptions. On many occasions, male colleagues have asked Jessica how her body handles constant travel, as if her gender makes her more fragile on planes? Her response has been that she's a marathon runner and in pretty good shape, yet she has been told to slow down, take better care of herself, sleep more, and take more personal time for herself.

Bonnie has experienced the same assumptions. She remembers a business trip in which the flight didn't get in until midnight. One of her male colleagues recommended pushing the start time back for the next morning's meeting.

"You're going to need some sleep," he said. Bonnie got up the next morning at 5 a.m. to work out, like she always does, and shocked the same male colleague when he saw her in the gym while he was on his way to get coffee.

Once again, women don't want special treatment. They don't necessarily want to slow down, sleep more, travel less, or have more time for themselves any more than any other person in a busy workplace.

**PUT IN PRACTICE**

The WIM can help by forcing the conversation about unconscious biases, and more importantly by being an example. Jessica had a leader in her organization who has always had a flexible schedule; he needed to be more available at home to support an ailing wife. When Jessica asked him, a very experienced professional, revered by other team members, to share his routine, she saw everyone breathe a sigh of relief. Here was proof someone could be highly successful and promoted without being chained to the office every single day. Here was a leader who people didn't assume was getting a special pass.

Achieving the goal of not singling women out, and not leaving men out, comes from creating a myriad of gender-free initiatives, from flex time to maternity/paternity leave.

In addition to offering real workplace flexibility, it's just as important to encourage employees to use these perks. Make sure there's no stigma or perceived retribution for anyone who wants to take advantage of these benefits, or an expectation that only women should use them. What better way to demonstrate this than having senior leaders (male and female) lead not only in policy, but also in practice?

Men can create change by being vocal. Think of the impact if a WIM tells his staff or colleagues, "I'm heading home; I have a standing appointment at six o'clock every night to have dinner with my family." Out of a thousand women polled in a survey, nearly 80 percent said they had *never* heard a successful man talk about balancing work with home.

To this point, Bonnie recalls a conference call with a group of senior leaders. One of the most senior leaders on the call was asked where he was on that day. He launched into a long explanation that he was "playing Mr. Mom" that day. He went on to explain that "of all days, his wife was out of town, and there had been a bomb scare at his kid's school." The subtext was that no one, especially a man, should work from home unless they have a darn good reason. It would have been powerful from a cultural inclusion perspective if he simply responded that he was working from home that day.

A WIM can also do the uncomfortable work of asking himself what might be keeping him from taking a stand or initiating change. One basic way the WIM can move the needle is to ask the women in his organization and company what it's like to be a woman there. As we mentioned previously, we can't expect men to completely understand what it feels to be a woman, but they can educate themselves. The only way to understand a problem is to talk to people involved in it and be truly open to listening to their perspective.

## WHAT'S THE POINT?

⚠ Women do NOT want special treatment; they simply want policies in place that are applied equally across genders. They do not want to be singled out. Well-intentioned support that applies to women only can actually hurt women at work, especially in discussions on advancement.

⚠ Women do NOT want to be selected/promoted because they are women; rather they want to be selected/promoted because they are capable and happen to be women.

⚠ Many men view gender-inclusion efforts under the guise of a zero-sum game in which they lose out.

## WHY IT MATTERS

△ Flexibility policies can be a great workplace enhancement when they are perceived to be appropriate for everyone—not just a specific group. Otherwise, there is the potential to hamper women from the start, creating perceptions about credibility and capability.

△ Not all women have the same desires, personal situations, or challenges. Don't assume based on stereotypes or bias. When in doubt, ask!

△ Flexibility is a win-win for everyone: men and women; employer and employee.

## WIMS: TIPS FOR ACTION

△ Model that it is ok to use flexibility policies by using them yourself—visibly and vocally.

△ Listen for comments in the workplace that suggest that people who take advantage of flexibility policies are perceived as less dedicated, committed, or promotable. Ask men and women what they need to have a more flexible and engaged organizational environment and take action for both genders.

# CHAPTER FIVE

# Please Let Her Finish

---

## WHAT HE SAID

In the workplace, across industries and geographies, women have a universal experience during meetings. A woman makes a valuable comment or proposes an idea, and it will be as if she didn't say anything. No response. The conversation moves on and a few minutes later, a man will make the same comment or proposal, and the rest of the room will back it up enthusiastically.

And then there are the frequent interruptions, sometimes referred to as "man-terruptions," because in many cases, it's men who interrupt women (although women are guilty of interrupting other women too). Bonnie recently experienced this when she commented on a topic in a meeting only to have a senior male leader in the meeting interrupt to say that he had a couple of comments to add to what she said. He proceeded to repeat almost verbatim—what Bonnie had just said, as if he didn't hear her at all.

An occasional situation like these is understandable—after all, we're all human—however, women report that these situations happen with a level of frequency that make the experiences confounding and maddening. It makes them question themselves, their clarity of message, and their ability to deliver it.

Another even more disconcerting experience for women is that of being shut down in meetings. Years ago, Jessica had just started at a new company and was in one of her first meetings. The topic for discussion was one with which she was intimately familiar. In the meeting with her newer colleagues, Jessica offered her insights and firsthand experiences. A senior male leader interjected, and told Jessica to bring her "listening ears" to the conversation instead of talking, because she was newer to the company. He told her it is always better to listen than to be heard.

### WHAT SHE HEARD

Jessica understood that a newcomer to any company should listen more than they speak—especially when starting out—but being shut down right from the start, particularly when she had a valuable contribution to make, clearly demonstrated to her that she was second class. It was humiliating.

Senior leaders who mentor and sponsor women in the workplace sometimes give them conflicting and confusing advice. If a woman doesn't talk at all in a meeting, she's coached that if she wants to be a part of the conversation and get noticed for her capabilities, she must speak up and lean in at the table. However, when she does speak up, she's sometimes told, "Tone it down. You're a little intimidating," or, "You come across as self-promoting," or, "You've got to listen more." Getting the right balance is a constant challenge for women. Men generally do not have to worry about these issues in meetings. When a man contributes with passion, conviction, and in a loud voice, he's judged as being knowledgeable and a strong advocate on the topic at hand. Men are also not interrupted or ignored in meetings nearly as much as women tend to be.

When a woman is constantly interrupted or her ideas are ignored in a meeting only to have the same idea proposed by a man a few moments later and it is championed, or she is shut down in a meeting, she receives the message that a woman's opinion doesn't matter.

## SO WHAT?

In the authors' experiences, as well as that of many of their female associates and colleagues, men are not interrupted nearly as much as women are during meetings. Women are interrupted constantly, by both men and other women. Over time, the impact of not being heard, being considered self-aggrandizing by speaking up, or being constantly interrupted is that women simply disengage. They lose confidence, they raise their hand less and less, and they avoid coming to the table unless they absolutely have to. It gets tiring when the loudest male voice usually wins; women who suffer from this communication fatigue end up picking their battles. In the end, companies lose because valuable contributions that could benefit everyone—and the bottom line—are lost.

In 2012, three women from Flynn Heath Holt decided to take a systematic look at the issue. They began by examining 360-degree feedback collected on 1,100 female executives at or above the vice president level—more than 7,000 surveys in all. They found widespread evidence in the executives' comments and in those of their colleagues and managers that meetings were a big stumbling block. They also surveyed 270 female managers in Fortune 500 organizations. More than half reported that meetings were a significant issue or a "work in progress." Finally, to get a picture of how the gender divide plays out in the highest-level meetings, they interviewed 65 top executives, including both male and female CEOs, from companies such as JPMorgan Chase, McDonald's, PepsiCo, Lowe's, Time Warner, and eBay.

In all of the research, both men and women agreed that meetings pose a concerning issue for most women. Tellingly, the male managers who were interviewed were well aware that women often have a hard time making their otherwise strong voices heard in meetings, either because they're not speaking loudly enough or because they can't find a way to break into the conversation at all. More than one-third indicated that when their female peers do speak up, they fail to articulate a strong point of view. Half said that women allow themselves to be interrupted, apologize repeatedly, and fail to back up opinions with evidence. Women surveyed, on the other hand, who are vastly outnumbered in many executive-level meetings and boardrooms and with few role models and sponsors, reported feeling alone, unsupported, outside their comfort zones, and unable to advocate force-fully for their perspectives in many high-level meetings.

As one said, "It's harder to read the room if there are no other women around the table."

The bottom line: men are rewarded for talking more, and women are not. In addition, women's ideas are also more harshly scrutinized.

Conditioning runs deep, and a strong, underlying sentiment remains in our culture that women are better to be seen and not heard. Many men are more accustomed to *looking* at women rather than listening to them. *Fast Company* recently published an article titled "What a Speech Coach Told Me About 'Speaking Like a Woman' (And Why It's BS)." The article acknowledges that women are often coached to speak differently to command authority and be heard at the table. Women are often told to work on their pitch and tone, to project more in order to show greater confidence, and to remove the personal touches that many women add to their speech. But linguists will tell you that female and male speech patterns have always differed. One of the biggest concerns that female mentees ask Jessica about is what to do with their voice; they fear they are too soft-spoken. And, they have been told that as a result of their soft voice, they are viewed as fragile and not strong enough for the "tough negotiations."

We need more women in leadership positions to acknowledge that those differences are really okay, and that it's not something to coach or to ask women to adjust or change. Rather, we must get more in tune to *hearing* women's voices, accepting women's speech patterns, and not associating tone with sincerity of message, strength, or capability.

Women in the workplace, including those in senior

leadership positions, are seen as more likeable if they don't speak up, express strong opinions, or take the initiative to have tough discussions when the situation calls for them. By not executing the same behavior that her male counterpart is rewarded for, a woman is viewed as a team player. What a woman hears is this: "Don't rock the boat, even if it's at the expense of you, your colleagues, and the company itself."

## PUT IN PRACTICE

A problem can't be solved unless it is first acknowledged. If a Well Intentioned Man can simply understand and admit that there's an issue with how women's communication is perceived by many men, then the road to change is possible.

Active listening is essential. In meetings, a WIM should observe when women are interrupted or ignored when they share ideas, and yet men who raise the same idea later are celebrated. Calling out the pattern will help to end this practice. When a WIM chooses to initiate these steps, the results will be better interactions and better decision making.

Jessica worked closely in the past with a male executive who began every meeting with "ground rules." One of them was a "no interrupting" rule. It was highly success-ful when it came to everyone having a voice and feeling heard, regardless of gender or position in the organization. Not only has Jessica adopted this rule to her meetings, she's also added a "no a-holes" rule—essentially, to respect every comment regardless of how different it is from your perspective—to ensure contributions are encouraged and valued equally.

A WIM can also encourage active participation from both genders. For example, if he's leading a meeting involving five men and one woman, it's important that he doesn't assume that if the woman doesn't speak up, that she has nothing to say. Soliciting her opinion will likely result in a valuable contribution. In the surveys mentioned previously, 30 high-ranking women were asked to name the one thing that they would change about how men treat them in meetings. Thirty-eight percent responded, "Ask us direct questions," or, "Bring us into the discussion." It may be counterintuitive, but good leadership involves seeking input from the quietest member(s) at the table.

At the risk of stating the obvious, one of the best things that organizations can do is to ensure that leaders invite more women to the table. When a woman walks into a meeting and finds that only 2 of the 15 people present are women, it takes a toll. Peer support and role models make a difference, as does developing a more robust pipeline of women in a visible and meaningful way.

## WHAT'S THE POINT?

△ Women are interrupted, ignored, or shut down implicitly—or explicitly—at an alarming rate in workplace meetings.

△ Women are often given confusing coaching to speak up but then to "tone it down." Meetings dominated by male counterparts remain a significant challenge for women to navigate.

△ The female voice stands out as atypical and out of the ordinary around the conference table because there are few, if any, women at the table.

## WHY IT MATTERS

△ Women have a unique perspective to offer, but they often disengage as a result of numerous experiences of being interrupted, ignored, or shut down.

△ Because women's voices aren't heard, and they stand out, they've become "otherized"—too high, too soft, or any number of other voice problems that women are perceived as having.

△ Women need men to hear women's voices!

## WIMS: TIPS FOR ACTION

△ Listen—truly listen—in meetings to observe if or how often women are interrupted and/or ignored. When you see it, say something.

△ Adopt a no-interruption rule in meetings and follow it with discipline. The culture will follow as well.

⚠ Engage the least talkative people or those with the softest voices at the table by seeking out their perspective and value differing perspectives. Actively pull them into the discussion, until they willingly jump in.

⚠ Help to increase women's contributions by adopting practices that focus less on the speaker and more on the idea. Leverage anonymous crowd-sourcing tools more often (just as orchestras use blind auditions).

# CHAPTER SIX

# Why Must She Choose?

---

**WHAT HE SAID**

Bonnie participated in a Stanford University executive program a number of years ago, which was made up of primarily male leaders with a sprinkling of female leaders. In one of the sessions, the instructor was reviewing and discussing the famous study on gender bias: the Howard/Heidi blind test.

At the end of the session, one of Bonnie's male colleagues turned to her and said, "So, which would you rather be?" Bonnie just looked at him, confused, and he continued, "Likeable or competent?"

"Why must I choose?" Bonnie replied.

The truth is at that time, Bonnie preferred to be competent versus likeable if she was forced to choose. But a woman shouldn't have to choose; after all, men don't face this choice.

Jessica had a similar experience. She had been hired to a new leadership position in the business following years as a successful corporate attorney, and her reputation as a tough negotiator had apparently preceded her. After less than six months on the job, a senior male leader told Jessica that she was too aggressive, not warm enough, and that she didn't care enough about people to be a good leader in the organization. Jessica was flabbergasted by the comment.

Not long after his stinging assessment, Jessica's team, peers, and manager completed a 360-degree review of her—the first review of her as a business leader. Her team, peers, and manager gave her management competencies and organizational climate the highest marks possible. She showed the results to the male leader who had criticized her as being too aggressive.

"You have this perception of me as an aggressive, cutthroat, ex-M&A lawyer," Jessica said, "but the people who work with me on a more regular basis view me as a visionary, people-oriented coach. How do you reconcile those differences?"

"I can't help the way I feel," was his response.

A light bulb went off for Jessica. She realized that there was nothing wrong with her or her leadership style. This male leader was unable to view her as both a good people leader—likeable—*and* competent. He couldn't rationalize that she could in fact be both.

### WHAT SHE HEARD

Many women regularly confront this double bind: if a woman is perceived as likeable, she's often not perceived as competent. Likeable aspects include being kind, easily influenced, nurturing, quiet, and helpful. She is assumed to be a team player and a willing backup that shies away from the limelight. Women who are dominant and decisive are generally viewed as competent but unlikeable.

Success and likeability are positively correlated for men, but they are negatively correlated for women. Sometimes, but not always, women are viewed as competent when they are more out-spoken and aggressive; in essence, when they embody stereotypically masculine traits.

Bain & Co. conducted in-depth interviews with 19 of the most senior women in consulting, private equity, and finance. They asked these women what strategies they adopted to navigate the gender imbalance at these senior levels. Many women felt pressure to adopt masculine characteristics in the office, and more than half agreed with the statement, "I often take on more masculine characteristics while at work." Sometimes this happens gradually and unconsciously. Nearly every woman found it challenging to thrive in a masculine culture while still feeling authentic.

Stereotyping permeates the workplace in other insidious ways as well. Women often end up doing the office housework. They're asked to take notes during meetings, or they volunteer to do so as a result of years of conditioning. Women often plan company events, whether they are assigned to do so or, once again, they volunteer. When a woman performs these tasks, she's viewed as a good sport and team player. Yet when a man raises his hand to take notes or to be on a planning committee, the response is to thank him profusely for volunteering, as though he's going out of his way.

## SO WHAT?

If a person needs to both produce results and be liked in order to get hired and promoted, a woman constantly faces a double bind. She can't be assertive and be perceived to demonstrate great people leadership. She can't be likeable and deemed strong enough for a promotion.

In many cases, women reach a certain level of leadership by being assertive, decisive, and strong. But once they reach these more senior levels, being assertive is considered no longer acceptable, and it holds them back. They're told they're not nice or soft enough, or not enough of a people person.

Adam Grant, in an article about this phenomenon, quotes a field psychologist:

> Male senators with more power, which is measured by tenure, leadership positions, and track record of legislation passed, spoke more on the senate floor than their junior colleagues, but for female senators, power was not linked significantly more to speaking time.

Grant's article, aptly entitled "Speaking While Female," discusses additional research in which it was found that male executives who spoke more often than their peers were rewarded with 10 percent higher ratings of competence. When female executives spoke more than their peers, both men and women, they received 14 percent lower ratings in the same arena. As this and other research shows, women who worry that speaking up will cause them to be disliked are not paranoid; they are often right.

Likewise, in a study done by psychologist Madeline Heilman, participants evaluated the performance of a male or female employee who did or did not stay late to help colleagues prepare for an important meeting. For staying late and helping, a man was rated 14 percent more favorably than a woman. When both declined, a woman was rated 12 percent lower than a man. Over and over, after giving identical assistance, a man was significantly more likely to be recommended for promotions, important projects, raises, and bonuses. A woman who helped got the same rating as a man who didn't help. The sad reality is that when women help others, they benefit less from doing so than their male colleagues.

Throughout Bonnie's career, she has typically been the younger leader supervising older, more experienced male employees. As a result, she learned to be tough and to hang with the guys. Over time, she learned that if she didn't want her point to be ignored or interrupted, she needed to be assertive in making her point.

Ironically, this assimilation to use a more assertive, masculine style that helped Bonnie rise to senior leadership is now often a stigma that she has to overcome, because she is viewed as aggressive or intimidating—despite great leadership feedback from direct bosses, subordinates and peers.

There is a difference between being assertive and aggressive, but people don't always distinguish between the two when they're forming an opinion about a female boss, colleague, or employee. When a man is assertive, he's viewed as having a strong opinion or being passionate. He's considered as someone who is confident and who knows what he wants.

Women are appreciated when they make bold moves for their companies, yet their likeability, and promotability, is tenuous if their approach is deemed to be too assertive. Often, at this juncture, a woman is also labeled as aggressive (with the associated negative connotations).

Matters get even more complex when it comes to succession-planning discussions and choosing candidates from inside an organization. Many times, the discussion about men includes all of the reasons why they will be successful in a role. The discussion about women includes all of the potential reasons they might fail in a role. In one such conversation, when Bonnie pointed out how differently men and women are considered, the participants in the discussion had clearly been unaware of the bias in their discussions—this is why it's called unconscious bias. Calling out the bias made it more conscious to all, and made it possible to change the conversation.

Research by the Catalyst organization confirms that despite numerous business contributions that women leaders have made, men are still largely seen as leaders by default. Researchers call it the "Think Leader, Think Male" mind-set because of the preponderance of men as leaders in the workplace. Because of this mind-set, women are faced with an impossible choice. They don't know whether to conform to masculine behaviors that may get them labeled too tough or to stay true to their feminine behaviors that may result in being seen as too soft or less than competent. To put it bluntly: women who want to reach for higher levels of leadership are damned if they do and damned if they don't.

### PUT IN PRACTICE

The Well-Intentioned Man can help women by paying attention to the subtle bias that occurs during meetings, such as who is assigned to take notes, to run the projector, to record the presentation, and to write on the whiteboard. He can suggest ways to distribute tasks more equitably and randomly. Also, most organizations regularly assess individual accomplishments and results. Why not recognize how the results are achieved as well—the acts of helping others and demonstrating teamwork to counteract the effects noted in the research above?

When a woman being discussed gets labeled as aggressive or

bitchy, a WIM can ask whether she is truly doing anything different from her male counterparts who are described in a much more favorable light. If the answer is no, then the WIM can speak up and ask why male colleagues aren't held to the same standard. Challenging a biased conversation, unfair generalizations, or inappropriate comments is critical and usually brings to light unconscious bias that would have otherwise gone unrecognized.

WIMs can intentionally shift conversations away from a discussion about gender and toward effective leadership traits. The truth is that organizations need a blend of masculine and feminine traits. When decisions are made based solely on the specific characteristics needed for a leadership role, the entire company takes a step forward toward gender inclusion and better business results. Similarly, if you're a WIM and you are in a leadership position, you can pay attention to what kind of leadership traits you select, promote, and reward. By doing so, you're likely going to learn about your own unconscious biases regarding the value of tough traits versus soft traits.

The "speaking while female" double bind harms organizations by depriving them of valuable ideas that women could contribute but may choose to hold back out of fear. Organizations need to find a way to root out this gender bias. Just as orchestras used blind auditions to increase the number of women who were selected, organizations can increase women's contributions by adopting practices that focus less on the speaker and more on the idea. By describing candidates based on their competencies and accomplishments without knowing their names and gender, bias takes a back seat.

One of Jessica's leaders, a WIM, once told her that he'd like to see the entire definition of leadership change. He wanted more executives who were caring and thoughtful. He didn't see those qualities as detracting from her—or anyone's—ability to take charge.

---

## WHAT'S THE POINT?

⚠ Women are regularly confronted with a double bind. If a woman is perceived as likeable, she's often not perceived as competent, and if she is perceived as competent, she's often not perceived as likeable.

⚠ Success and likeability are positively correlated for men, but they are negatively correlated for women.

⚠ Regarding promotability, discussions about men include all of the reason why they will be successful in a role. The discussions about women include all of the potential reasons they might fail in a role. This is often unconscious!

## WHY IT MATTERS

⚠ Women are appreciated when they make bold moves for their companies, yet their likeability and promotability is tenuous if their approach is deemed to be too assertive.

⚠ Women are often disadvantaged in succession planning discussions because the discussion is biased.

⚠ Women are faced with an impossible choice—conform to masculine behaviors that may get them labeled as too tough or stay true to themselves that may result in being seen as too soft or less competent.

## WIMS: TIPS FOR ACTION

⚠ Pay attention to the subtle bias that occurs toward women during the career discussions. Is the discussion consistent between male and female employees who are being discussed? Pay attention to the way you recognize and reward things like teamwork for men and women, and make a conscious effort to be consistent.

⚠ When a woman under discussion gets labeled as aggressive, a WIM can ask whether she is truly doing anything different from her male counterparts who are described in a much more favorable light. Intentionally shift conversations away from a discussion about gender and toward effective leadership traits.

# CHAPTER SEVEN

# Women Can't Have It All, But They Can Do It All

___

The title of this chapter was chosen based on a talk given by a CEO of a well-known accounting firm. During this female CEO's speech, she suggested that the term "having it all" means different things to different people, but most of all, it's a judgment, whether from the media, the feminist movement, or someone you know. In the end, she told the audience, each woman has to decide what is right for her in matters of personal and professional life, and how she'll blend the two.

Women constantly face criticism from others about their

choices. If they stay home to take care of the kids, they're judged. If they work and put their kids in day care, they're judged. If they take time off, there's more judgment.

When women discard what everyone else thinks, and decide what "having it all" means for themselves, then they can in fact "do it all"—but in their own way, and in their own time. In a recent *Forbes* commentary piece titled "Female Company President," Katharine Zaleski suggests that women can't have it all, but they can have what matters. And every individual woman is at a different place in her journey with trade-offs to consider. This reinforces the point that what women want must not be generalized and should not be assumed.

In a hiring consensus meeting, Jessica and a group of senior level male leaders were discussing candidates for an important position that required a good deal of travel. The majority of the male leaders immediately ruled out one of Jessica's suggested candidates because she had young children. They automatically assumed she wouldn't want to travel. Yet as the discussion deepened, everyone realized that this woman was the most qualified person for the job and best fit for the team. It turned out that she did want the position, and now she has it.

## WHAT HE SAID

More than a decade before this book was written, a bright young supervisor who reported to Bonnie came into her office. She had worked at the company for 10 years. She was extremely nervous and on the verge of tears as she told Bonnie that she had something important to discuss. Finally, the young woman announced that she was pregnant.

Bonnie excitedly told her that was great news, and asked, "What's wrong? This should be a good thing!"

The supervisor told Bonnie that four years prior, when she was pregnant with her first child, her male boss was extremely negative upon learning the news. The boss told the young woman that he was concerned about whether she would remain committed to her job. He wanted to know how much time she was going to need off and what projects he could or couldn't assign to her. The entire conversation was centered around the inconvenience of her pregnancy on the work team.

As a result, this woman (like many others) had been dreading the conversation with her new boss, Bonnie, about her second pregnancy.

This young woman's experience was by no means uncommon. Prior to writing this book, Bonnie and Jessica surveyed their joint network—a group of women that they have gotten to know personally and professionally. Participants were asked to describe what was holding them back at work. One woman replied that she wanted to both excel in her career and have children. However, she said, "I never tell people that I work with that I want children." She feared that the assumptions about her level of commitment to work and her desire to be a mother would keep her from being assigned to key projects or prevent future promotions.

That response could have been written 30 years ago, and yet women still face this challenge today. At work, in order to be taken seriously, women still feel like they're under a gag order when it comes to discussing their desires about home and family, especially if they desire to climb to higher levels in their workplaces.

## WHAT SHE HEARD

Women hear that pregnancy is bad news when they're met with disapproval from superiors after telling them about their happy news. When opportunities are limited due to maternity leave or having a young child, women also internalize the experience. Women suffer a crisis of confidence when their career aspirations are limited in this way. They all too often assume that it is their lack of talent or qualifications that are hindering them. In many cases, they set out to work harder and to demonstrate their competence and commitment, when the issue is really one of unconscious bias about whether a woman can be a mom and a committed employee and leader. Imagine how absurd that would sound if men's commitment to work were constantly challenged simply because they became fathers.

Back to the survey of the authors' women's network: another question that we asked women was "What is the worst advice you've ever been given at work?" One of the most jaw-dropping responses was from a woman whose male colleague had counseled her not to take a job that required extensive travel because her husband might be unfaithful when she was gone. It's incredible to think that a woman would have to even consider that a role at work would require sacrificing her marriage.

## SO WHAT?

Many of today's senior male leaders grew up in a generation with family situations in which their fathers had a career and their mothers stayed home with the kids. Assumptions and biases about what women can and should do in the workplace spring from the environments that these decision makers were raised in and what was normal for them. It is important to note that we are not judging men who fit this description. Bias in and of itself is not bad. In fact, we all have biases. They only become problematic when we are unaware of them or when we believe that they are 100 percent true and when we allow them to guide our behaviors.

Another response in the authors' survey highlights how upbringing can guide assumptions and biases. A male colleague told one participant that he was reluctant to invest in a college education for his daughter because she was a girl and it was going to be a waste of money. He assumed that she was going to get married, opt out of the workforce, and be taken care of by her husband. It's difficult to believe such assumptions still exist in the twenty-first century, but they do.

Assumptions exist not only about a woman's value in the workplace, her commitment to work if she wants a family, and whether she can balance family and travel; they also exist about her ability to show up regularly and stay focused. Many workplaces are stuck in the mind-set of the twentieth century, when the traditional way of measuring job commitment was based on whether an employee was the first one in the office in the morning and the last to leave at night. Despite our huge leaps in technology, many leaders possess a bias that if you're not visible in the office daily, then you're not working as hard as everyone else. We all know this isn't true. It's 2017.

Another typical mode of thinking is that the more demanding a job is, the less likely a woman is to want it. However, that's absolutely not what the data shows. A Gallup study found that women who aspire to leadership positions are unlikely to be deterred by the demands of the job. Other research indicates that gender doesn't affect job commitment. Leaders might assume that women, especially mothers, are not willing to take on all-encompassing senior management roles. They might believe that women don't want to pursue leadership positions.

However, in Gallup's latest report *Women in America: Work and Life Well-Lived*, data shows that women are interested in advancing to the top. Forty-five percent of working women say they would like to become CEO or have a position in senior management or leadership. A slightly higher number of working men (54 percent) say the same. And when asked how serious they are about obtaining such a role, women are just as likely as men to say they are "extremely" or "very" serious: 69 percent versus 68 percent, respectively.

Another study was conducted of 25,000 male and female Harvard Business School graduates who had similar career priorities. Upon graduation, the women in the study rated opportunities for career growth and development as a slightly higher priority than the men. As time went on, the female participants who opted out of work did so as a last resort because they felt stuck in unfulfilling jobs with limited advancement opportunities. The majority did not opt out in order to have families. It dispels the notion that the primary reason that women leave workplaces is to have a family.

Research conducted by Bain & Company shows that men and women begin their careers with similar aspirations and equal confidence about reaching top management. New employees aspiring to reach top management were actually higher for women at 43 percent and men at 34 percent. Confidence to achieve it was on par for men and women with respondents indicating confidence at 28 percent and 27 percent respectfully. After a few years into their career, however, women's aspiration fell 27 points to 16 percent and confidence of achieving it fell 14 points to 13 percent. Men's aspiration to achieve top management remained the same at 34 percent and their confidence fell only three points to 25 percent. This example starkly contrasts women's confidence and aspiration once they have experienced the workplace. According to Bain research, three critical factors influence this drop in confidence among more experienced women:

1. They don't see themselves fitting into the typical stereotypes of success within their company.
2. Their supervisors have not been supportive of their career aspirations.

3.  They do not have role models similar to them in senior or top management positions in their company.

Research shows that men and women are more likely to act the same way in job involvement and mobility when they are in similar jobs. The false belief that women leave jobs faster comes from the fact that across the board, women are concentrated in lower-level jobs, where greater turnover and absenteeism exist because of a lack of opportunities and challenge in those positions.

The reason we don't have more women in leadership is a result of workplace biases limiting opportunities that lead to women settling for lower-level roles or opting out due to a lack of clear paths to advancement. The situation causes the behavior, not the other way around.

**PUT IN PRACTICE**

One of the most important, and simplest, things a Well-Intentioned Man can do is to ask questions rather than making assumptions. For example, a couple of years ago, Bonnie was in a meeting about creating a pipeline of talent for senior-level positions. The process involved identifying individuals with the potential to become department heads or executives within the next 10 years.

No women were listed among the candidates. Bonnie told the room it was difficult for her to believe that in their entire organization, not a single woman existed who could achieve department head or higher in the next decade with the right development. She began going through the organizational chart and asked why one talented female employee wasn't being considered.

One of the male leaders replied that he had discussed advancement with a talented woman but that she had told him that she was happy doing what she was doing.

Bonnie told him to consider that the employee might not have a lack of aspiration, but rather a lack of belief in what was actually possible. Bonnie asked the male leader to go back and have a deeper conversation with the woman. When he did, he discovered that she in fact desired a higher-level position but that she didn't believe the opportunities would be extended to her. When she was told that company leaders believed that she had the capability to move up with the right development, she was eager to be considered.

Previously in this chapter, the story about the woman with young children who was automatically discounted as a candidate for a position requiring travel was shared. When assumptions were questioned and it was discovered that she did want the position, she found a way to make it work.

Her family hired a nanny, and she and her husband trade off traveling for work. A WIM should never underestimate a woman's ability to find a way to "do it all."

Actions that Well-Intentioned Men can take to create more gender inclusion aren't complicated or difficult. It's more about shutting off the autopilot and guarding against biases that try to guide the way.

A WIM who is in a position to create and schedule company events can consider changing them up to be more inclusive. Some companies choose not to have spontaneous happy hours anymore but instead hold family social events. Women (and men) with families can plan ahead and participate instead of being considered aloof because they can't join in with the team down at the bar.

The WIM can also acknowledge that today's workplace is stuck in the past, designed primarily for men who are married to homemakers or to women who handle the majority of the household tasks. To bring the workplace into the present, a WIM can create a variety of schedules and career tracks that make it easier for women to grow instead of opting out. One solution could be a work week that involves being in the office four days and at home on the fifth. Work doesn't have to take place within eight hours during the day, either. Such flexibility lends itself to taking care of children or aging parents. This will not only help to prevent women from opting out but will help men who would like options too!

Leaders are initially uncomfortable, and understandably so, with not treating everyone the same. But cookie-cutter approaches don't work in the long run. Instead, structuring jobs based on individual goals and needs help to bring out the best in employees and in the company.

It's been stated before, but it bears repeating: when a WIM calls out bias in meetings in front of other men, it sets a standard to be followed. Think about the last time a man was asked how he was going to manage his career after he had children. In career and selection discussions, a man's power to make unconscious biases conscious cannot be underestimated. As the saying goes, if you see something, say something!

## WHAT'S THE POINT?

△ When opportunities are limited due to maternity leave or having a young child, women internalize the experience. Women suffer a crisis of confidence when their career aspirations are limited in this way.

△ Bias in and of itself is not bad. In fact, we *all* have biases. They only become problematic when we are unaware of them or when we believe that they are 100 percent true and we allow them to guide our behaviors.

△ Research shows that men and women begin their careers equally confident about reaching top management (actually more women aspire to it than men), but women's confidence and aspiration declines with experience.

## WHY IT MATTERS

△ The reason we don't have more women in leadership is a result of workplace biases limiting opportunities that lead to women settling for lower-level roles or opting out due to a lack of a clear path to advancement.

△ Research dispels the notion that the primary reason that women leave workplaces is to have a family, so it is possible to change the trend.

## WIMS: TIPS FOR ACTION

△ Ask questions rather than making assumptions about what employees want or what they are willing to do.

△ Create a variety of schedules and career tracks that make it easier for women to grow instead of opting out (and make them available to men too).

△ Call out bias in meetings in front of other men and set a standard to be followed.

# CHAPTER EIGHT

# Prove It (Again)

---

## WHAT HE SAID

Jessica always thought she'd leave the practice of law some-day, because for as long as she could remember, she wanted to follow in her father's footsteps and work in the busi-ness. How that would eventually unfold was fuzzy; Jessica had never made a concrete plan. Due to the reshuffle of a pending acquisition, and much earlier in her career than she envisioned, a senior male leader offered her a position running a regional sales team in Latin America.

Instead of being thrilled, Jessica tried repeatedly to talk the senior vice president out of the job offer. She told him that she was too young, that she was not qualified, and that despite speaking fluent Spanish, she had never used her language skills for work. On and on Jessica went, describing all the reasons, as a corporate lawyer, that she wasn't qualified for the job.

For weeks, she stalled and intently tried to disqualify herself.

Finally, the male leader affectionately said, "You're not a dumbass. You'll figure it out." He refused to take no for an answer, and made it plain that Jessica's options were to either take the position or leave the company. He clearly believed that she was capable for the role.

Jessica took the job, and it was one of the best decisions she ever made. Today, she's grateful to have had such a powerful advocate in her corner. At the time, however, she lacked the confidence and vision for her career. Like many women, Jessica didn't see that because she was talented and possessed a strong work ethic, and she had transferable skills, she would figure the job out. Unlike men, most women believe that they must possess every prerequisite before pursuing a new challenge, and Jessica was able to check very few of the boxes at that point.

One of Jessica's former colleagues works for a public company that recently had two candidates in the final round for the important position of chief financial officer. One was male and the other was female. Both were excellent, well-qualified candidates. During his interview, the male candidate told the board that he wouldn't stay at the company if he didn't get the job. The female candidate told the board that she would support whatever decision was made and that she was committed to the company.

The male candidate got the job.

It's a generalization, but men are confident while women suffer a lack of self-confidence unless they are able to check off every prerequisite for a specific role. Men often position and promote themselves for a job before it is even posted. Women rarely take the same approach, and the ones who do often receive feedback that they are viewed negatively as self-promoting (as Chapter 5 highlighted). In addition, as in the CFO interview above, a woman may apply for a job, but she will not likely put the same pressure on the company to be selected as a male candidate. Often, the woman is satisfied with merely being considered for the role.

Women's general lack of confidence about aiming high and going after opportunities stems in part from a multitude of experiences in which male counterparts' performance and potential are assumed to be better than women's.

Ben Barres, a previously female neurosurgeon who decided

to have a sex change at the age of 40, highlighted this phenomenon best when he shared:

> Shortly after I changed sex, a faculty member was heard to say, "Ben Barres gave a great seminar today, but then his work is much better than his sister's work."

And also,

> Men tell me things that I don't think they would have told me when I was Barbara. A neurosurgeon at Stanford told me that he has never met a woman surgeon who is remotely as good as a man. Another told me he thinks women are like small children. Many have told me that they think gender stereotypes are generally true.

**WHAT SHE HEARD**

When a woman learns of a new job opening, or she is encouraged to apply for one by a boss or colleague, the first thing she hears is her own internal voice telling her that in order to apply, she must have every qualification box checked off. Even if she's proven herself in her current position, she believes she must prove herself again to be considered.

She's not entirely incorrect in her assessment. If she's

bringing different skills to the table than other candidates, such as an ability to excel in communication or proven ability to collaborate well across organizational boundaries, those skills may not be valued as much as technical skills and experience. Instead, they may be seen as soft female-oriented skills or skills that don't equate with the traditional organizational culture's view of what a leader is (male).

Many women end up not taking risks. They falsely believe that if they keep their heads down and work hard, their contributions and abilities will eventually get noticed. Countless examples prove, however, that this is not necessarily what occurs.

But again, women are faced with a double bind. When women do advocate for and position themselves, they're often criticized for being self-promoting. Or worse: they're labeled as ambitious. For women, ambition and drive are often perceived as bad things. It's not fair, but it's true.

Companies that want to excel need to view ambition in women with the same positive lens as ambition in men. Leaders should ask themselves how they can encourage and maintain that hunger in women and not view it as a negative to be quelled.

## SO WHAT?

A study conducted by Hewlett-Packard found that men do not think twice about applying for a job for which they are less than fully qualified and underprepared, while fully qualified and overprepared female candidates hold back.

One of the takeaways is that women feel confident only when they believe that they are perfectly prepared. Many men comfortably fly by the seat of their pants during meetings, with little or no familiarity with the topic at hand, while a woman would rarely put herself in that position. Early in her career on the business side, Jessica took comfort in overly preparing for everything. It gave her confidence where she felt she lacked in years or experiences.

It would benefit women to adopt an "I'll figure it out" mentality. Approximately a decade ago, Bonnie's boss promoted her to a position running a business in a foreign country. When he informed her of the promotion, Bonnie told him she was unsure whether she was the best qualified person for the job. His response was that if he didn't think Bonnie was qualified, he wouldn't have put her in the role.

During that time period, the same boss connected Bonnie with an executive coach. As a result of their conversations, Bonnie realized that she had been holding herself back. Her true desire was to rise to a senior executive level, but she hadn't believed it was possible. Verbalizing the aspiration made it possible for Bonnie to create a plan to achieve it, which included letting others around her, especially those who could help, know of her aspiration.

Recently, when the CEO of a renowned consulting firm had an opening on her executive team, nine men expressed interest, but zero women did, even though a number of qualified female candidates were available.

Women often hold back from pursuing leadership promotions, and men often overlook them despite the fact that a study by Zinger and Holcomb, who wrote the book *Inspiring Leader*, found that women excel at leadership skills when rated by their peers, bosses, direct reports, and associates. The ratings were based on 16 competencies of leadership. The two areas where women outscored men to the highest degree were taking initiative and driving for results, which have long been thought to be male strengths.

The one area where men outscored women was in the ability as a senior-level manager to develop a strategic perspective. At first glance, that might appear to be the reason for why more women don't get promoted into senior-level roles. But as the study's authors dug deeper, they found the results to be skewed. Since more men are concentrated in these senior roles, the results were weighted toward men, not women.

Bias is both subtle and deeply impactful. Facebook has taken the lead in working to end gender bias in Silicon Valley by making their training on the issue public. In one case study from the company, two copies of the exact same resume were presented for evaluation. On one resume was a man's name, on the other, a female's name. With no difference in qualifications, 80 percent of people deemed the man worthy of the job compared to less than half for the woman.

Performance attribution is another area where bias rears its ugly head. When a man performs well in a task or situation, it's often attributed to his natural ability or his intelligence. When a woman performs well, it's attributed to hard work, a great mentor, or even luck.

Women unconsciously collude with this by refraining from highlighting their talent, attributing, for example, a job promotion to being in the right place at the right time. Men, however, generally do not discount the results brought by their innate brilliance. In a study of several thousand male and female political candidates, all with the credentials to run for office, men were 65 percent more likely than women to believe they were very qualified to run. *Sixty-five percent.* That's a stark difference.

## PUT IN PRACTICE

Unfortunately, countless men, even well-intentioned ones, wonder, *What fault is it of mine that women don't put themselves out there? Why is it my fault that women don't speak up? Why is it my responsibility to urge them to do so?*

Gender bias is not men's fault, but it will not and cannot change without their help. It's not solely about doing the right thing or being a good person. Gender inclusion creates stronger teams, companies, and ultimately, global economies. Without gender inclusion, companies will not remain competitive. And if gender bias is not surfaced and consequently mitigated, then gender inclusion will not improve.

With women still underrepresented in high-level positions, it's important for male leaders to seek them out and find out why they're not applying. Push them.

In 2016, Justin Trudeau, the prime minister of Canada, created a campaign called "Invite Her to Run." It was designed to bring more women into his cabinet. The campaign invited men and women across Canada to urge women that they thought were qualified to run for office. The effort was spread across social media and other channels. As a result, Trudeau now has the country's first-ever, gender-balanced cabinet.

As a Well-Intentioned Man, Trudeau didn't take no for answer. To bring his trade minister aboard, it took quite a bit of arm twisting. She eventually agreed.

Bonnie has a friend in the United Kingdom who was being urged by friends and local politicians to run for the elected mayoral position in her city. The friend was hesitant for all the reasons highlighted earlier, including believing that she needed every prerequisite, as well as wanting to be loyal to a male colleague also in the running. She finally did run for the office. Her decision came only because of the efforts of her support system and allies pushing her to admit that she wanted it.

The bottom line: women need support in order to advance, and they may not even know it. When WIMs encourage high-potential women, their reluctance can be overcome, especially when they always wanted the opportunity but never thought it possible.

We know we're putting the Well-Intentioned Man in an awkward position by suggesting that, like Trudeau, they shouldn't take no for an answer from a qualified female candidate. By doing so, he can help her rise to the occasion. If he does have his own concerns about her ability to lead, he can ask himself if his perceptions are based in reality or on assumptions. He can seek to understand her underlying reasons for holding off, such as fear of disrupting a family schedule or fear that putting herself out there will lead to disappointment.

A Well-Intentioned Man in a leadership position can seek to create a team with many perspectives different from his own. John Maxwell describes the building of a diverse team as building a dream team in his book *21 Irrefutable Laws of Leadership*. Questions to ask when determining whether you have a dream team are: Does my team contain introverts and extroverts? Male and female perspectives? Long-time employees as well as newcomers with fresh perspectives? These questions can identify areas where a different perspective is missing and can help to create a team so well rounded that its decisions benefit the team because the quality of the decisions will be significantly better as a result of the diverse perspectives.

A simple yet powerful way the Well-Intentioned Man can help women is to advocate for them after they obtain a leadership position.

For example, after Jessica was put in her first significant leadership role in Latin America, the vice president who hired her sent around an e-mail to everyone she would be working with. It described her attributes and qualifications. By sending one e-mail, he boosted her credibility in a big way and helped to dispel any questions about her competence before people met her. Endorsement opens doors.

It's important for a WIM to question his own beliefs about the capability of women. One way to do this is to examine whether he is hiring people based on his own comfort level. For example, Jessica was part of a three-person panel interviewing three job candidates for a position. The other two interviewers on the panel were men. The makeup of the candidate pool was the same: two men and one woman.

After the interviews, the men on the panel told Jessica they preferred the male candidates because of the ease of the conversations during the interviews. However, a good part of those conversations had centered on a mutual love of soccer, a sport in which the female candidate had little knowledge. Jessica pointed out to her fellow interviewers that the woman wasn't necessarily a bad fit; she simply didn't possess the shared interest. A light bulb went off; the male interviewers told Jessica she was right.

Bonnie once heard a CEO say, "I would never put somebody in an important position if I didn't personally know them." That's understandable. However, if you're a man who isn't making a conscious effort to interact with women in your organization, you're never going to know them. Therefore, they're never going to be perceived as people that you could trust enough to hire them for important roles. Water-cooler talk counts. It builds relationships. The WIM can explore and expand the people with whom he engages at the office.

In addition, WIMs are highly effective when they consciously take on mentoring and sponsoring of women. Such a sponsor persistently affirms that a woman belongs in a male-centered organization. He coaches her to take full ownership of her accomplishments and contributions to team projects. He also repeatedly encourages her to take risks. Men truly don't realize the onslaught of cultural messages that women encounter every day that deter them from striving for or feeling comfortable seeking high-level positions.

In turn, a mentor can ask a woman what she can do differently to advance, such as whether her confidence level is apparent to others and if not, how she can express it. When she does take risks, he can counsel her to focus on all the reasons that she might succeed, not all of the reasons that she might not. Confidence builds when worst-case scenarios are examined. More often than not, a woman realizes that her fear is illusory, a monster in the closet. Jessica recently mentored a high-potential woman who suffers greatly from a lack of confidence. Even though Jessica and this woman's male leader are certain that she is ready for that next step, this talented woman doesn't believe it.

Together, Jessica and the WIM are focusing on clear, tangible experiences to give to the woman that will allow her to prove to herself that she is in fact ready for the next level.

Years ago, Bonnie's boss suggested that she talk to his peers about moving out of her human resources role and into one leading a business. She discussed the position with five male leaders, and she was told, discouragingly, that while her background was interesting, she needed engineering and manufacturing experience for them to consider her for roles in their organization.

Bonnie talked to one more person: a female vice president. The vice president told Bonnie that she needed to recognize and banish her inner critic. She said that if Bonnie obtained a role on the business side, she could use her many transferable leadership skills to be successful. She reminded Bonnie that as a great leader, all she needed to do was find an engineer who would be more than willing to explain everything Bonnie needed to know about designing and manufacturing a product. She also advised Bonnie that once she succeeded in one of these business roles, Bonnie's background would no longer be questioned.

The WIM can offer similar advice to women suffering from imposter syndrome, which runs rampant even among highly successful females.

> **Imposter syndrome** (also known as **imposter** phenom-
> enon or fraud **syndrome** or the **imposter** experience)
> is a concept describing high-achieving individuals who
> are marked by an inability to internalize their accom-
> plishments and a persistent fear of being exposed as
> a fraud.

Procedural changes within organizations also help to create parity. For example, if recruiters set standards before the recruiting process begins, it's more difficult to allow unconscious bias to take over. They won't be swayed by affiliations around gender or by common interests such as sports. Figuring out the best fit before the process begins is the way to go.

Another way organizations can raise awareness of gender bias is to require a second set of eyes on performance evaluations. Software even exists today to assess evaluations—as well as job postings—for bias.

Organizations also can implement a new step to their hiring process, one where hiring decisions are evaluated. When an executive can explain objectively and credibly why a candidate wasn't selected, questions of bias are assuaged. If the decision maker cannot justify his or her decision based on qualifications and objective criteria, perhaps hidden bias was involved and could be brought to light. In any event, a process where leadership decisions are discussed openly leads to heightened awareness. Transparency goes a long way toward building trust.

One of the best things that organizations can do as well is exactly what happened to Jessica at the beginning of the chapter: change the conversation from "Who is the best person for the job?" (i.e., has checked the most boxes or has the most tenured experience) to putting candidates in positions to build the right team. This framing can help managers to look for people with various and diverse strengths and not just those who remind them of themselves or the picture of who has traditionally held a particular role.

---

## WHAT'S THE POINT?

△ Women feel confident only when they believe that they are perfectly prepared for a new position, while men will generally go for it even if not completely prepared.

△ Women excel at leadership skills when rated by their peers, bosses, direct reports, and associates, and they outscore men in the competencies of taking initiative and driving for results, which have long been thought to be male strengths.

△ When a man performs well in a task or situation, it's often attributed to his natural ability or his intelligence. When a woman performs well, it's attributed to hard work, a great mentor, or even luck. This is performance attribution bias.

## WHY IT MATTERS

⚠ Many women end up not taking risks. They falsely believe that if they keep their heads down and work hard, their contributions and abilities will eventually get noticed.

⚠ Women make great leaders and should not be overlooked. They bring to the table many strengths, including taking initiative and driving for results, which have long been thought to be male strengths.

⚠ Performance attribution bias causes women's perceived capabilities to be minimized.

## WIMS: TIPS FOR ACTION

⚠ Seek out women for specific roles and find out why they're not applying. Push to understand whether they really are not interested or whether they are holding back out of fear of disappointment or lack of belief that it is possible.

⚠ Instead of asking, "Who is the best person for this job?" ask, "How do I put the best team in place? What perspective is missing?" This framing can help a WIM look for people with various and diverse strengths, not just people who remind them of themselves or the picture of typical candidates in the role.

⚠ When assessing performance for men and women, consciously consider whether you actually rate performance objectively—or whether potential unconscious bias seeps into the process.

⚠ Listen for gender bias in discussions about performance and potential—if the conversation about men and women differ, call it out and help the organization to learn about and make bias conscious versus unconscious. Only when it is conscious is it possible to mitigate it.

# CHAPTER NINE

# It's Never That Time of the Month

———

**WHAT HE SAID**

During one discussion at an executive leadership training that Bonnie attended, a female Stanford professor shared research around gender diversity. Another male attendee brought up the common perception discussed previously in this book, that women are viewed as either likeable or competent, but not both. In many cases, the male attendee added, they're viewed as bitchy and emotional, "especially that time of the month."

Everyone in the room dropped their jaws—especially his male colleagues.

None of the four other women in the room said a word.

Bonnie was outraged and challenged the colleague. She stated that she didn't think he could ever respect, promote, and sponsor women in his organization if he possessed an underlying belief that denigrated them.

His reply, "I'm just telling you what I see with the women in my life."

Two decades earlier, Bonnie had a similar experience, but this time with a female colleague. Bonnie was having challenges with her supervisor and felt he neither listened to nor respected her. She approached a human resources professional in the organization to discuss the situation. Bonnie was articulate, professional, and eager to learn what she could do differently to connect with her superior.

The HR person responded to Bonnie's inquiry with, "Is it, by chance, your time of the month?"

Bonnie was shocked. She responded by saying that she had a real challenge to discuss. Yet she was still told by the HR person, "When emotions run high, it's often because it's that time of the month."

Casual joking about women being emotional during

menstruation can permeate women's lives, particularly in homes where husbands, fathers, and brothers humorously bat around the "time of the month" phrase. Unfortunately, that legitimization has seeped into the workplace.

Menstrual-cycle inquiry goes hand-in-hand with women being labeled as too emotional—among the many harmful stereotypes about women. Bonnie recently held a gender-diversity training session for men and women leaders along with another female colleague. The session began with asking participants to call out descriptors representing male and female stereotypes. The men in the group immediately shouted out in unison "emotional" as the first attribute they associated with women.

Negative assumptions are tied to the perception that women are purely emotional, not rational, beings. Those assumptions include the belief that women are unable to handle stress or to make fact-based or tough decisions. Compiling these assumptions, women may not be viewed as capable of having the tough career assignments that are complex, high pressure, and that require significant negotiation. These are the same positions, however, they are often regarded as essential to ascend the corporate ladder and prove readiness for the top jobs.

## WHAT SHE HEARD

The assumption that women are too emotional infiltrates the work experience. For example, Jessica has received feedback on her style that she "wears her heart on her sleeve." The feedback almost always arrives after she makes a strong point, such as in a meeting where her position was backed up with facts and data. However, when male colleagues take a similarly strong, well-researched position, rarely are they deemed as too emotional. As a result of the feedback pattern, Jessica has started to ask (male) colleagues which part of her point, whether made in a meeting or via e-mail, contains emotion. The response is generally a long pause as the light bulb goes on.

Bonnie heard this same "wears her heart on her sleeve" comment during a review of employees' potential for leadership. One female employee who was discussed was deemed a high performer and top producer who repeatedly exceeded expectations. Yet as the discussion intensified, one of Bonnie's colleagues said that this employee "wore her heart on her sleeve," and he wasn't being complimentary. When Bonnie asked what he meant by the phrase, the colleague replied that when the employee disagreed or gave challenging feedback, her face and body language portrayed negative emotion. Bonnie responded by pointing out that his observation was not precisely in sync with the meaning of the phrase. Earlier in the same conversation, a male employee who was also a high performer was described as "not having the best bedside manner, but he's really good," using the same description of face and body language as the female employee that was viewed as "wearing her heart on her sleeve." Calling out the difference in the way the male and female employees with same face and body language were being described so differently was a learning opportunity for everyone involved in the discussion to realize how people unconsciously view men and women differently.

The flip side of this emotional stereotype is when a woman attempts to adopt an emotionless leadership style, she's often labeled an "ice queen." In the early days of Bonnie's career, her motto was to "never let them see you sweat." She was all business and was careful to maintain a strong boundary between her personal and professional lives. Bonnie was repeatedly told that colleagues and superiors found her professional manner cold. She was coached to loosen up and "let her hair down."

Men can express extreme emotions (we can all think of screaming matches, hanging up the phone, and even, as Jessica recalls, throwing things at each other), but women are criticized and unfairly stereotyped for showing any emotion. It causes women to be viewed as weak. Angry men are viewed as powerful; angry women are, again, viewed as emotional. The authors both have observed a number of male colleagues whose style is to get in people's faces and scream to make a point. Some use profanity as a power play. While in today's workplace, this is less common, the point is that men are rarely viewed as emotional—even when they are in fact behaving in an emotional manner.

Bonnie recalls one executive in a tense negotiation with a third party. On a break, the executive told the team that he was going to pound his fists on the table and insist that this latest offer was final or that he was finished negotiating. This behavior would most assuredly not have been viewed as rational or acceptable if it were demonstrated by a woman.

### SO WHAT?

Research by Dartmouth professor, Dr. Ella Bell, has found that a preconceived notion exists that women tend to get too personally invested in their work. Jessica has received that feedback. One of Jessica's core beliefs as a leader is grounded in caring for the people who work for and around her. She finds it beneficial both for their well-being and engagement as well as the company's effectiveness as a whole. Jessica has asked herself: What is negative about investing in the work you do and in the people who do it with you?

Studies show that women are more relationship focused,

and this engenders higher levels of engagement. A Gallup poll found that employees of female managers were on average 6 percentage points more engaged than those working for a male manager. In fact, employees with female managers outscored those with male managers on 11 of 12 measures of engagement. Nevertheless, countless companies continue to place great value on traditionally male attributes such as aggressiveness, competitiveness, and individuality. They may, however unintentionally, punish characteristics that demonstrate so-called female traits: collaboration, cooperation, and nurturing. Jessica has been described as a "mother hen" with her teams for showing compassion and empathy to individuals.

Those traits are often labeled as weaknesses. Code phrases used to prevent advancement include saying that the individual, man or woman, "doesn't have the intestinal fortitude" to make tough decisions or take a stand on difficult issues.

Research, however, tells a different story. Women are better at managing complexity. Research shows that when complexity rises, men focus on fewer inputs, and thus the quality of their decision making drops, while a woman's remains high. Also, it is counterintuitive that women are viewed as categorically worse at negotiating than men. Have you ever seen a mother negotiate for her child at school? She knows no fear. Research shows that when a woman is negotiating for someone else, whether her kids, her friend, or her colleague, she is a tougher negotiator than most men.

A couple of years ago, one of Bonnie's colleagues inappropriately berated her team during a meeting at which Bonnie was absent. The team contacted Bonnie afterward to express their dismay. Bonnie promptly initiated a face to face discussion with her boss and the offending colleague, during which she expressed her concerns. At the end of the conversation, however, Bonnie's boss summed up the meeting as a "cathartic experience." By labeling it as such, the entire conversation was framed as an emotional one, causing Bonnie to wonder if he thought that she had blown the colleague's behavior out of proportion.

The moral of the story is that women are constantly perceived as too emotional, although this is not grounded in concrete evidence. Difficult and even crucial conversations are viewed through a clouded lens. In the service of attempting to have an important dialogue, women are often dismissed as emotionally driven.

**PUT IN PRACTICE**

The Well-Intentioned Man can start to shift the workplace by being aware that the "too emotional" stereotype exists for women, and it generally isn't true. If a woman is behaving inappropriately or if she takes a strong position on a topic, then a WIM should discuss it with her in the same way that he would discuss it with a man—focusing on facts and data attributed to behaviors, not gender, and definitely not on "that time of the month."

Meanwhile, the WIM can also gauge how we as a society view emotion in general. For example, women who are labeled as emotional are often seen as acting aggressive. But men dubbed as emotional are often admired for getting in touch with their feelings—for being in a state of growth. Or even worse, emotional outbursts by men are tolerated as a demonstration of passion about a subject.

If a WIM finds himself labeling or calling a woman out for being emotional, he can pause and ask himself: *Why do I think that? If a man were demonstrating the same behavior, would I label him as overly emotional?*

Reflection may bring a different answer than the original assumption.

The WIM can also overcome any reluctance that he might have to providing women with honest feedback for fear of igniting a strong emotional response. From the time they are young, men are taught not to make the opposite sex cry and not to cry themselves. Yet many of us have had women and men cry during performance reviews or during highly charged work situations. Everyone wants honest feedback (even if it is difficult to hear) provided that the feedback is being given for the benefit of the individual's growth and development.

One of the most powerful tools a WIM can employ in an emotional situation is to simply listen without trying to solve the issue or keep a lid on it. Tears often provoke discomfort for people. This may seem like unusual advice, but the authors recommend keeping a box of tissues around. Rising from your desk to locate them is a good way to buy time as you deal with your own unease and as you formulate your response. A measured response is always better than one given off the cuff that may come across as insensitive.

We all have discomfort with giving and receiving feedback. Research shows that men often receive feedback based on performance, while women receive feedback based on personality traits (like being empathetic and caring). One suggestion for organizations is to create a continuous debrief culture where feedback and courageous conversations don't feel so personal. Set performance expectations both before and after events. If organizations define the expectations, what roles people will play, and the measures of success before a meeting or project kicks off, it facilitates a follow-up discussion, grounded in facts and measurable outcomes rather than allowing bias to seep in. Everyone being on the same page from the beginning regarding how outcomes will be measured is always best, regardless of gender. Always ask, "How can I/we do this better?" If this is a constant question in organizations, it will drive feedback based in facts rather than preconceived gender perceptions.

A workplace devoid of emotion is a workplace devoid of authenticity. Making it acceptable for women—and men—to show emotion creates an environment of trust that benefits everyone.

---

### WHAT'S THE POINT?

⚠ There are a multitude of phrases such as "that time of the month" that hinder women's advancement and play to the perception of women as highly emotional beings.

⚠ On the flip side, if women do not show emotion, they are often viewed as cold and unapproachable.

⚠ Men who express extreme emotions are often viewed as authoritative or powerful without being seen as emotional, even when they are in fact behaving in an emotional manner.

## WHY IT MATTERS

△ An unemotional and robotic workplace would be miserable for all involved! But by singling out one gender as the emotional one, it forces everyone toward a cold standard that's impossible to reach.

△ Due to the emotional stereotype, women are often left out of crucial feedback conversations.

△ When women attempt to have crucial conversations, the entire conversation is often painted with an emotional brush, and key team-wide or company-wide feedback is dismissed.

## WIMS: TIPS FOR ACTION

△ Rely on and seek out facts and data grounded in behavioral attributes rather than gender-based assumptions.

△ Ask yourself, *if a man reacted the same way, would I view the reaction as emotional or weak?*

△ Strive for your organization to create a debrief culture, setting clear expectations before and after, so that feedback doesn't feel so personal. Personify the courageous conversations—it isn't personal. It's business.

# CHAPTER TEN

# That's Actually Not a Compliment

---

**WHAT HE SAID**

Jessica was at one time the first female leader in a visible role in Latin America. At the end of her first full year, it was time for her performance review. Jessica had knocked it out of the park in her new position, exceeding every metric that her team's contributions were measured on. She received the highest rating on the rating scale.

Yet her boss' compliment to her wasn't about the strong results, her outstanding employee engagement, or her initial success in a fix-it role. Instead, he told Jessica that she had accomplished a great deal and had done well for **being the first woman** in that key role in Latin America.

Bonnie has had similar experiences in two different performance reviews. In the first, her male boss said that her performance had been excellent despite the demands on her time from becoming a first-time grandmother. In the second review, her boss noted that although Bonnie had experienced numerous health and family issues throughout the year, she had met his expectations, which were exceedingly high.

In a similar vein, Jessica, while leading a sales team, was told by a colleague that she was "much more commercial" than he expected her to be. When Jessica questioned the statement, her colleague told her, without thinking twice about it, that there aren't many commercial women in our business, so he didn't expect her to "get it."

### WHAT SHE HEARD

Many male leaders and colleagues are completely unaware of the multitude of backhanded compliments that they deliver to female direct reports, colleagues, and even bosses. The impact of Jessica's boss's statement about her was not only demeaning, but it was confusing. Had she accomplished a lot for being a woman? Or had she accomplished a lot based on the fact that her metrics exceeded targets?

Bonnie wondered: would her performance have been

considered excellent if she hadn't gone through the challenges and demands on her time? In addition, Bonnie pointed out to both her boss and a human resources director that it was unlikely that a male colleague's performance review would have discussed the impact on his work from being a first-time grandfather.

Pooling experiences, both Bonnie and Jessica have reviewed and completed thousands of employee performance evaluations. Neither has ever seen personal issues mentioned in men's reviews, although they appear in women's. Men's evaluations are solely about performance and accomplishments.

The intention of both bosses in these stories was most surely to convey positive, even admiring, feedback. But neither Jessica nor Bonnie felt valued and praised for what they had provided—outstanding work.

### SO WHAT?

Compliments with an underlying gender bias result in feedback that is qualified. In fact, the authors have found that, more often than not, a qualifier is unfailingly attached. "You did a great job...*for a woman.*"

These backhanded compliments are so entrenched in our culture that they often go unrecognized. Actor/writer/

producer Tina Fey points out the phenomenon perfectly in her book *Bossypants*. Fey writes:

> What is the rudest question you can ask a woman? *How old are you? What do you weigh?* No, the worst question is: *How do you juggle it all?*

Asking how you're juggling it all assumes that you may be doing everything, but you're not doing any of it well. It's perceived as a way of saying, "What are you failing at?"

Bonnie's response to male colleagues asking her how she managed taking care of her family, tending to the home-life demands, and performing at a high level while making it to senior leadership is to say that she has a great, supportive husband and couldn't do it without him. Jessica's way of disarming the backhanded compliments is to use humor. When "How do you do it all?" or "You do too much" is lobbed, Jessica says simply, "I fooled you!"

In the workplace, women also consistently receive comments and compliments about their appearance. As a meeting is about to begin, Jessica has been greeted with conversation starters about her appearance such as "You dress so well" or I like your shoes/haircut/outfit/jewelry." It's off-putting to receive feedback in a professional environment that has nothing to do with your capabilities, and that subtly (or not) undermines your performance and even brain power. Unfortunately, both men and women convey such comments to female colleagues, so much so that it has become acceptable.

The authors themselves used to communicate this way with other women, but they have made a conscious effort to stop, recognizing that our society's unhealthy emphasis on appearance has a subsequent negative impact on women. The lens has to shift, and women must model that shift too.

The #LikeaGirl ad campaign lays bare the impact that the terms "run like a girl," or "throw like a girl" have on girls, whose self-esteem plummets at puberty, according to research. Such pejorative terms erode confidence and initiative. Behaving like a girl should not be an insult, and the campaign has released a new video. Its intent is to empower young women and attack the self-esteem crisis that permeates many of their lives. "Why can't 'run like a girl' mean 'win the race'?" asks the video. It will be a great day when phrases like "Woman up!" are as common as "Man up!"—and when phrases invoking the feminine exemplify a call for strength, success, and power.

**PUT IN PRACTICE**

WIMs should begin to notice their casual language and

evaluate whether it is unintentionally offensive to women. Comments or compliments that focus on appearance should be scrapped, so should work feedback that has "for being a woman" tacked on the end.

No woman wants to feel that every decision or evaluation that her leader makes about her involves consideration about gender ("Wow, for being a woman with three kids, she does a great job!"). She wants to be recognized solely for her accomplishments, achievements, and how well she gets the job done—just like her male counterparts.

In addition, a WIM should find a way to connect with women beyond their appearance. By doing so, the chances of being perceived as friendly and professional are much greater than the chances of being perceived as offensive.

Again, because these ways of communicating are so prevalent in our society, blame is not being placed on men. It sounds overly simplistic, but thinking before you speak can have a tremendous impact. Many colleagues routinely address a group as "guys" even when a woman is present. Unless men start to think about it, the language won't change.

Diversity training teaches that if gender is important to the conversation, then, by all means, use it. But if it's not necessary in the conversation—if specificity is not required—then it's best to leave it out, including phrases such as "May the best man win," "Act like a man," "Just take it like a man," and so forth.

Little efforts add up over time, changing what is at first awkward to eventually become the norm. Women notice and appreciate it when leaders make efforts to introduce gender-neutral phrasing, such as "chairperson," into workplace communication. Intention is valued, even when it results in humorous situations. For example, Bonnie has received e-mails with the salutation: "Gentleman and Lady." Jessica has received, "Gentlemen and Jessica." Though, it could be argued that Bonnie is much more of a lady than Jessica—*wink!* The authors suggest a simple "Colleagues" would do.

Meanwhile, many women are reluctant to speak up when backhanded compliments occur or when they receive feedback with gender bias. They don't know how to point out the issue for fear of being perceived as overly sensitive or emotional. After all, women don't want their counterparts to think, "Can't she just accept a compliment?"

We all need to engage in and foster courageous conversations around these topics and the unintentional bias that exists in the workplace, as that is really what these backhanded compliments represent. These conversations help. In addition to seeing it in action, research shows that having these conversations can lead to results on a broader scale. As just one example, research has shown that when biased comments are made about female political candidates ("She's got great legs"), the female candidate suffers in the polls. If, however, the female candidate calls out those comments for what they are (backhanded compliments that detract), her poll results improve.

In the authors' experience, when the communication is called out in the right spirit, with the question of whether a man would be described or approached in the same way, a light bulb goes off. They haven't seen resistance, but rather a realization that men didn't even realize they were doing it—it was unconscious. When women highlight the communication problem without blame or judgment, most men genuinely appreciate it.

Workplaces can help employees by encouraging open-dialogue sessions about communication issues. A free-flowing conversation in a safe environment can do wonders toward taking a company to a new level regarding the identification and elimination of bias. Such dialogue serves to position men, who comprise the majority of decision makers in companies, to become allies and advocates. Awareness that allows for mistakes to become learning opportunities brings progress and eventually culture change.

---

## WHAT'S THE POINT?

△ Compliments with an underlying gender bias result in feedback that is qualified, and therefore not a compliment.

△ Women often don't speak up about backhanded compliments for fear of being labeled as weak, sensitive, or emotional.

△ Casual language is often male-oriented and excludes women—but again, speaking up about it places a woman in danger of being seen as difficult or too sensitive.

---

## WHY IT MATTERS

△ Women want to be recognized for performance and capability—period.

△ Women do not want their gender to be persistently a part of their feedback—whether positive or negative. They want to be viewed as a professional.

△ Women want to be able to engage in conversations about inappropriate language without being labeled as sensitive or the issue being deemed a women's issue.

## WIMS: TIPS FOR ACTION

△ Think twice before commenting on women's appearance in the workplace, even if the objective is a simple conversation starter. Focusing too intently on something such as a woman's outfit can subtly undermine a discussion on performance and even brain power.

△ Call out backhanded, albeit well-intentioned, compliments. There is so much power in having a WIM address these comments to start to change the workplace dynamic.

△ Foster courageous conversations on gender-related communication issues in the workplace with open-dialogue sessions in a safe environment.

△ Ask women in your organization about common, well-intentioned compliments that are not really compliments from their perspective.

# CHAPTER ELEVEN

# She's Not Really Sorry

---

**WHAT SHE SAID**

A succession planning meeting was about to take place, which included a review of Bonnie's career potential. Bonnie carefully crafted a note to two male leaders: her boss and another executive who had been acting as one of her sponsors. She asked them to advocate for her in the discussion if given the opportunity because she wanted to ensure that the impact of her contributions and desires were apparent.

But before Bonnie sent the note, she forwarded it to Jessica for feedback. Jessica quickly pointed out that Bonnie had begun the note by writing, "Sorry to be so forward about this..."

"Why did you say you were sorry?" Jessica asked. "You're not sorry."

Bonnie reminded Jessica how often she has received feedback that she's too aggressive and can be perceived as self-serving. She had inserted the obligatory apology to soften the request, humble herself, and convey likeability.

## WHAT SHE HEARD

Jessica reminded Bonnie that there was no reason to apologize for anything and that the apology would likely have an unintended effect. Many men perceive apologies as a sign of weakness, uncertainty, and a lack of confidence.

Unfortunately, women undermine themselves both personally and professionally when they constantly apologize for themselves. Shampoo brand Pantene played off this widespread experience with a YouTube ad that portrayed scene after scene—from work meetings to casual situations at home—of women apologizing for inconsequential actions.

Many women feel the same way Bonnie did, that they must

apologize for advocating for themselves, or they use it as a way to soften the message.

## SO WHAT?

Qualifying language pervades women's speech in the workplace. Using the word "just" is another example. Phrases such as "I just want to check in" or "I just think..." unintentionally come across as either apologetic, tentative, or both. "I want to check in" is a clear statement of intention and, it demonstrates confidence. "I think x, y, and z" lets people know where you stand.

Women also frequently use the word "actually" as in "I actually disagree" and "I actually have a question." While intended to take the edge off a request or comment, the impact is that a woman sounds slightly surprised. Meanwhile, when women use the word "think" instead of "believe"—"I think we should launch the new product"— men mistakenly believe they are weak in their commitment or evaluation.

Finally, women routinely preface opinions with phrases such as "I'm not an expert on this, but..." or "I know you've been thinking about this for a long time, but..." The goal is to dismantle any potential sting in the feedback. But, by unconsciously using tentative wording and language, women are perceived by their male colleagues and leaders, even WIMs, as unsure of themselves. Or, they're put back into the too-emotional category.

Softened-up communication is rooted, again, in the double bind that so many professional women have at some point found themselves in. They receive conflicting feedback. A woman is told that she is either too weak or too strident; abrasive and bitchy, or incompetent.

One woman's experience in finding her a way out of the double bind is described in the book *Talking from 9 to 5: Women and Men at Work* by linguist Deborah Tannen. The story is about a female surgeon who was one of the few women in her specialty. At first when communicating with nurses and staff, she attempted to mimic the barking, directive, military-style speech of the male surgeons who had trained her. The approach backfired. No one would listen to her. Effectiveness came only after she began treating staff with respect and warmth without diminishing herself.

**PUT IN PRACTICE**

The story of the female surgeon illustrates the premise that remains that if a woman is having a challenge at work—from communication to behavior to dress—it is the woman who needs fixing.

The Well-Intentioned Man can help to change that paradigm by highlighting qualifying or apologetic speech in the same way that Jessica did with Bonnie's succession-planning communication. He can ask, "Why are you sorry about that?" He can remind everyone that no one needs to be an expert to have a good idea.

While women do need to take the time and energy to self-correct apologetic language, the Well-Intentioned Man can turn the tables and drain the judgment out of what is currently considered weak communication. He can approach his female direct report, colleague, or boss about an issue with, "Sorry to bother you. Just wanted to check in: what do you think we should do?"

Most importantly, the Well-Intentioned Man can recognize the double bind that women often find themselves in. Particularly if he is in a position to promote a woman or her initiatives, he can recognize that qualifying language doesn't mean that she isn't confident in her ideas or her positions. She is simply caught between conflicting forces.

Along the same lines, organizations need to recognize that men and women do speak differently. The goal, especially initially, is not for women to replicate how men speak or communicate in order to be seen as having more confidence in their perspectives. Organizations, many led by WIMs, need to consider the linguistic differences in tone, language used, etc., between men and women, and be alert that although women are accustomed from an early age to use language to soften the blow, it is not an accurate reflection of their confidence or conviction in the matter at hand.

## WHAT'S THE POINT?

⅄ Qualifying language pervades women's speech in the workplace—women have been conditioned to precede statements with words like "sorry," "just," and "actually."

⅄ The goal for many women using this qualifying language is to soften the message and to ensure that they are not received too harshly.

⅄ Women are conditioned to soften the impact of their opinions—as though having an opinion is stepping out of line.

## WHY IT MATTERS

⅄ Women are perceived by their male counterparts as vague, lacking confidence, or lacking expertise, whereas women who don't use qualifying language are often labeled pejoratively and seen as too harsh.

⅄ It's too easy to fall back on the old stereotype of women being too emotional when they state their opinions plainly.

## WIMS: TIPS FOR ACTION

⚠ Call to light and challenge apologetic language that conditions a belief.

⚠ Leverage apologetic or conditioned language as well in order to turn the tables on this use being a gender-related qualification.

⚠ Linguistically, women and men are different. Share this research with your organization and catch yourself when coaching women to sound more like men.

# Conclusion

───

While the subject of this book is complex, the purpose of it is simple: to make unconscious gender bias more conscious. It is only when we make biases more conscious in our daily interactions that we can make a dent in its troubling impact in the workplace.

"I AM A RAVING CAPITALIST," writes Jeffery Tobias Halter, in his book *Why Women: The Leadership Imperative to Advancing Women and Engaging Men*. He reminds us that growing revenue, improving operating profits, and enhancing company reputation are all obtained by increasing the number of women in organizations and in leadership. His objective in writing the book was to create courageous conversations in organizations to drive business results. The significance of the business impact cannot be ignored.

The first step toward gender inclusion is to become aware that women's actions and communication styles are often misinterpreted. Assumptions (and bias) are developed about women, and erroneous conclusions are drawn about their aspirations, abilities, and capacities for leadership. Even if assumptions are sometimes true, they are rarely if ever 100 percent true, so allowing them to guide decisions—consciously or unconsciously—is inherently unfair and harmful.

Hopefully, whether you are reading this book because a woman in your life bought it for you, or you have a female family member that you want the best for, or you are simply interested in opportunities to improve your business results, you learned something from the many stories and research supporting this issue. If so, then you have probably also reflected on some of the actions that you can take to recognize your biases (we all have them) and to improve gender inclusion. Absolutely every one of us has a role to play— male or female—in this journey.

Perhaps, you aren't even male. In writing and revising this book, the authors received an extraordinary amount of feedback from women as well. Women that get it, and know that despite all of their best efforts, without men at the table, we can't move the needle on gender inclusion.

It is the hope of the authors (and thousands of women

in workplaces globally) that this book will be leveraged by leaders and human resources professionals as it was intended: as a field guide to steer real-life examples and to spur tangible actions and to fully engage Well-Intentioned Men in courageous conversations.

Many men have crossed the bridge and gained a better understanding of the workplace experience for women. Corporations have increased their training on this topic of gender diversity and inclusion as well as unconscious bias. Facebook has even gone so far as to make its training public, as it recognizes that this is too important of a topic to keep internally (https://managingbias.fb.com). Employee resource groups and women-in-leadership conferences abound. And even to some extent, policies have become more gender friendly. All of these efforts have been helpful and educational.

But the needle hasn't moved substantially: women are still the minority in nearly every leadership scenario. Why? Because companies can't legislate or impose the essential organizational culture change that must occur. It has to be voluntary. And behavior change is only possible when beliefs shift. It is the mission of this book to compel the Well-Intentioned Man, to evaluate his beliefs and to shift them based on his renewed or heightened understanding of the decades-old challenge of gender bias in the workplace—and more importantly, the benefits of improving gender inclusion.

Common sense is a powerful tool. Opportunities are easily illuminated when a Well-Intentioned Man takes a step back and asks himself to consider what his proposal, request, or assessment would be in any given situation if he were dealing with a man rather than a woman. Policies, practices, and procedures are important, but thoughtful examination trumps them all. Men have tremendous power to radically transform the workplace for women, and when they engage that power in everyday interactions, the workplace will change. Then it will be a man's—and a woman's—world, and we will all benefit!

# About the Authors

---

## BONNIE J. FETCH

 Bonnie is a wife, a mother, a grandmother, a senior leader and a Chicago native. Bonnie began her career in the service industry running full service restaurants and then owning a small family business. She then joined a Fortune 50 company where she has held a range of positions with increasing global responsibility in logistics, manufacturing, product design, human resources, organizational development and business leadership. Bonnie has lived and worked outside of the U.S. and has traveled extensively on 6 continents,

spending a significant amount of time in Europe and Asia. Bonnie holds board and officer roles on several privately held for-profit company boards. Bonnie holds a Bachelor of Science degree in Applied Organizational Management with postgraduate studies in leadership and organizational behavior. She graduated from the Stanford University Executive Program in 2011 and attended the Singularity University Executive Program in 2015.

Bonnie believes strongly in serving the community in which she lives and works, and she has served on nonprofit community boards that serve women, children and families in need. She founded two local chapters of professional societies and diversity councils, and she serves as an executive sponsor for a women's initiatives network. She was awarded *Illinois' Most Powerful and Influential Woman* award in 2011 and *25 Women in Leadership* award in 2015. Bonnie has spoken passionately at many conferences and events aimed at developing men, women and organizations on topics including: the value of diversity and inclusion, discovering unconscious bias, and creating an engaged and inclusive work environment.

## JESSICA D. POLINER

 Jessica began her professional career as a generalist corporate lawyer in growing, acquisitive public companies. She worked for a law firm and three Fortune 200 companies as an in-house lawyer before successfully transitioning to business and management positions with increasing responsibilities in a Fortune 50 company. As a business leader, Jessica has worked in sales, marketing, distribution, mining, operations, and governmental affairs. A Hungarian by ancestry and arguably also in spirit, Jessica has spent most of her career working, traveling and living outside of the U.S., with significant time in Central and South America and India, and speaks at least three languages fluently. Jessica attended Vanderbilt University for her undergraduate degrees, studied at the Universidad de Buenos Aires, attended law school at Marquette University on a St. Thomas More scholarship, and recently completed classes in design thinking, iterating and prototyping at IDEO-U.

Jessica is a passionate community advocate and has served on various local and global Boards. She volunteers her time outside of the office with organizations focused on youth education and women's empowerment. She was the recipient of a "Future of Change Award," and also received a "Forty under Forty" award in 2009. She was most recently featured in an article entitled: "Jessica Poliner: On the Move, In More Ways than One." Jessica is a member of various professional women's organizations and was also nominated to an executive professional organization by the Panamanian government. She is an active member of various diversity and people councils, founded the first women's employee organization group in Latin America, serves as an executive sponsor for various women's initiatives groups, and developed and teaches curriculum on personal branding and building women leaders outside of the U.S. Jessica's worked with various public, private and governmental organizations and speaking engagements on women in leadership, cultural integration, and championing diverse and inclusive teams. Her passion for these subjects knows no limits, and she is eager to leverage this book to help other organizations.

Made in the USA
Columbia, SC
29 November 2018